Praise for *Write a Must-Read*

"When you are ready to embark on the Artist's Journey and write the book you were called to write, read *this* book. AJ Harper's *Write a Must-Read* is itself a must-read, an essential resource to help you produce the works you were put on Earth to bring forth."

STEVEN PRESSFIELD, bestselling author of *The War of Art*

"If you want to write a book everyone talks about, this is the book that will show you the way. *Write a Must-Read* is honest, empowering, and actionable."

MIKE MICHALOWICZ, *Wall Street Journal*–bestselling author of nine books, including *Profit First*, *Clockwork*, and *Get Different*

"If you want to write a nonfiction book, *Write a Must-Read* must be the first book on your reading list. It will also be the only book you'll need. AJ Harper is the rare writer who can translate the complex craft of writing into a gripping, easy-to-digest narrative. If you want people to buy your book, read it, finish it, act on it, and then tell everyone they know to buy it, then buy this book now. It's simply the best book on how to write a book people want to read."

MICHAEL PORT, *New York Times*–bestselling author of nine books, including *Book Yourself Solid*, *Steal the Show*, and *The Referable Speaker*

"There are plenty of editors who can help you write a good book. There are plenty of writers who write books you envy. And then there is AJ Harper, who not only understands the entire craft of writing, but has developed a process that delivers consistently great books for her author clients. If you want to write a book that changes lives, read *Write a Must-Read* first."

PAMELA SLIM, award-winning author of *Escape from Cubicle Nation*, *Body of Work*, and *The Widest Net*

"Even after having worked with AJ Harper on two books, reading *Write a Must-Read* encouraged me to do more of the most important thing: Get to know my reader even better. Reader First isn't just a philosophy. It's a step-by-step process to write the must-read book your readers are waiting for you to write."

JEFFREY SHAW, author of *LINGO* and *The Self-Employed Life*

"This is an extremely useful guide for nonfiction authors who want their books to make a difference, instead of merely serving as branded merch. I'm going to recommend AJ Harper's book to my clients."

WILL WEISSER, editor and ghostwriter

Praise for AJ Harper's Top Three Book Workshop

"AJ Harper is the David Foster of the book-crafting business. David, a world-renowned musician, composer, and record producer, has won sixteen Grammy Awards. Artists with whom he's worked have remarked that in addition to his raw musical talent, David's true genius is in his ability to pull out of the musicians he works with the depths of what they're capable of creating. Among her many other gifts, this is AJ's talent as well. There is a delicate balance in holding the space for someone while they strive to do their best creative work without letting them get overwhelmed or lose hope. I am a much better writer, a better creator, a better person for having had this incredible experience."

SUSIE DEVILLE, founder/CEO, Innovation & Creativity Institute; author of *Buoyant*

"I like to think I'm a process-driven person. I also have a fond appreciation for efficiency; in fact, I've built multiple businesses around it. But for some reason, when I signed up for AJ Harper's Top Three Book Workshop, I thought I was just going to sit down and crank out some words that would come together magically and become life-changing for people. I was wrong. AJ forced me to slow down and think about writing differently, using a process I had never considered before. One that wasn't really about me. One that was about the reader. First. Last. And always.

Her process forced me to slow down to start to feel what I was writing. It turns out that it was what I needed—not to barrel through like my instincts told me, but to think it through like my author-brain told me. When it was all said and done, I knew I would have a great book—because that's what AJ helps people do—but what I got was more than that. It was more than I had ever imagined, actually. It was me. It was my voice. It was my destiny. My future. The writing process that AJ taught me not only made me an author, but it also made me a better one. One that will continue to impact the world one book at a time."

KASEY COMPTON, founder, KC Consulting; author of *Fix This Next for Healthcare Providers*

"I'd never written before. I went into AJ Harper's program cold turkey. It was amazing. Learning the whole process, getting the knowledge and information written, then having the process at my fingertips and being able to go back and utilize that information ... it improved my business—which tripled. Writing this life-changing book helped me serve my clients better, which helped my business grow. It catapulted me to where I wanted to be."

DAVID RICHTER, founder, Simple CFO Solutions; author of *Profit First for Real Estate Investing*

"I know how to write a book. I've been a professional writer all my life. I've written articles and posts and copy and even some books. But I was shooting in the dark. Now, there's light. I will not only write this book, I will write future books."

SARAH THURBER, managing partner, FourSight; co-author of *The Secret of the Highly Creative Thinker*

Write a
Must-Read

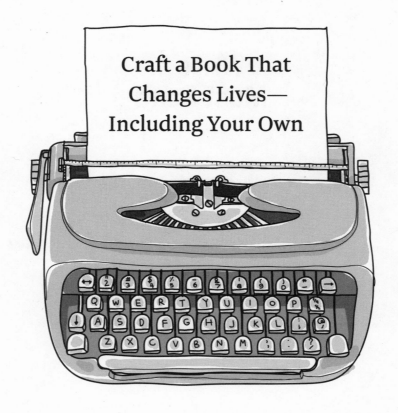

Craft a Book That Changes Lives— Including Your Own

Write a Must-Read

Cataloguing in publication information is available from Library and Archives Canada.
ISBN 978-1-989603-69-7 (hardcover)
ISBN 978-1-989603-70-3 (ebook)

Page Two
pagetwo.com

Edited by Amanda Lewis
Copyedited by Tilman Lewis
Proofread by Alison Strobel
Jacket design by Peter Cocking
Interior design by Setareh Ashrafologhalai
Indexed by Donald Howes
Printed and bound in Canada by Friesens
Distributed in Canada by Raincoast Books
Distributed in the US and internationally by Macmillan

22 23 24 25 26   5 4 3 2 1

ajharper.com

For Jack.

If there's a book that you want
to read, but it hasn't been
written yet, then you must write it.

TONI MORRISON

Contents

Introduction
A Book Is Forever

WHEN I WAS a ghostwriter, my motto was, "A book is forever. Write a good one." So many clients came to me because they wanted to "just get something out." Knowing how much effort, time, and money is involved in writing, publishing, and marketing a book, even a mediocre one, I wondered why anyone would start the process with that attitude.

I wrote exclusively for personal and professional development authors: books that promise to help readers improve some aspect of their life or work. The "better business card" racket that dominated my industry at the time—and still does—created a "drive-thru" mentality about books. I imagined wannabe authors driving up to the menu at Books-to-Go and ordering their debut: "I'll take a two-hundred-and-fifty-page business book, Tony Robbins style, with a side of Brené Brown. Hold the action steps. And can you super-speed that? I need it in seven minutes, not ten."

I once had a client hire me to write her second book. When I asked about her first one, she said, "Oh, please don't read it. It's just a little thing I wanted to get out." Please don't read it? She had a book out there that she didn't want people to read. Can you imagine? She counted on the fact that no one would crack it open, because she wrote it in a hurry so she could say she was a published author. She wasn't proud of her book; she knew it could have been better—much better. And yet, it was still available for anyone to purchase.

Click on the listings for many Amazon category bestsellers and you'll see a lot of "abandoned" books—books that people wrote and published quickly and then left up for proof that they wrote it. How can you tell? Look at the reviews. Has it been a year or more since someone left one? That means the author likely isn't promoting it, or not much. Look at the sales rank. Is the book ranked at one million or higher? That means it sells a handful of copies a year.

How did this happen? How did we get to this place where the main goal is speed, not quality? Where the focus is on the perks of being an author, not authorship?

In 2005, when I shifted from writing plays to ghostwriting books, most of the people I met just wanted to add a book to their platform. Sure, they wanted it to be good. Yes, they hoped it would help some people. But their primary goal was to get their book done and use it to catapult their careers and businesses. They wanted higher speaking fees—or they wanted to become a speaker. They wanted to drive clients to their business. They wanted to become an influencer, a brand, a big f-ing deal. And they believed a "better business card" book would help them do all that. They didn't expect their published work to be on par with the books they loved. Heck, many of them didn't expect people would read their books. That strategy worked somewhat for some of them. But it would have worked better if they'd written a better book.

I later learned that the "better business card" concept was born after self-publishing became more accessible, affordable, and accepted, and with it came a legion of people who profited off aspiring authors. These people and companies touted the speed and ease of self-publishing and, in doing so, dropped the editorial standards and necessary milestones followed by traditional and high-end hybrid publishing. Authors churned out books in months, even weeks. And when they didn't have time to write their own books, or didn't know how to write, they hired ghosts like me to do it for them.

Over the next ten years, I worked with more than five hundred authors—some for just one chapter, others for one or multiple books. I had the privilege of writing for and with some of the most successful authors of that time. And I noticed a pattern. Those who focused on their reader—their desires, their questions, their concerns—had legions of followers. Those who focused on themselves—their message, their ideas, their stories—did not.

You can game the system to become a bestselling author. You can even legitimately pull it off at launch. But what happens to your book after it's published? You won't gain a massive readership if people don't read, love, and recommend your book.

Here's the thing many aspiring authors don't understand (yet). Any book *will* help you expand your career and grow your business. If you want the catapult, though, you need a must-read. A great book, a truly transformational book, a book that really does change lives, *that* is the book that will get you the highest and best results. You know why? Because people will talk about it. It really is that simple. Why do successful thought leaders have legions of fans? Because they wrote a book that made such an impression on readers, their readers told a friend. Or a colleague. Or a family member. They said to one or more people, "You've got to read this book." And they said that because the book helped them in some way.

Your book is not a better business card. Why would you want that? People throw business cards away. Don't write a book to promote yourself. Write a book because you have something to say that could really help people. Period. If you go into writing a book with the intention of "just getting it out there," you are not going to write the book you were meant to write or help as many people as you could.

A book is forever. Once it's out there, you can't get it back. Every book printed has a life of its own. It's on bookshelves, in boxes, on garage sale tables. It's given as a gift. Your kids will read it. Your grandkids will find it and read it. Strangers will read it. Future clients or employers will read it. Writing a book is a major endeavor, so why shortchange yourself and your readers by trying to rush through it? Why not make it great? Why not write a book that really makes a difference?

I hope that's why you're reading this right now—because you *do* want to make a difference. That's the first requirement to write a must-read.

IN 2016, burned out after writing too many books and feeling disillusioned by the self-help industry, I hung up my ghost costume. Some of my clients encouraged me to teach or coach aspiring authors so they could write their own transformational books. At first, I was reluctant. I thought, *No one else can do what I do. It's intuitive.*

When I shared this belief with Mike Michalowicz,[1] with whom I've written nine books, including *The Pumpkin Plan*, *Profit First*, *Clockwork*, *Fix This Next*, and *Get Different*, he called me out. "That's bullshit. It's your ego talking. You have a system, and you can teach that system to other people. You just need to break it down."

Impossible. Most people don't want to put in the work it takes to write a must-read.

Then Mike asked me to attend an author retreat in Maryland and provide support for the attendees. He'd teamed up with Michael Port, author of the bestseller *Book Yourself Solid* and other books. Again, I was reluctant. I had worked one-on-one with my ghostwriting clients over months, sometimes years. How could I help these people over the course of four days?

I don't remember how it happened, but I ended up doing back-to-back laser coaching to help the aspiring authors with their core concepts and their outlines. To say I was winging it would be an understatement, but I approached it the same way I wrote game-changing books. I figured out how to help each author in their own language. I drew on the clarifying questions I had asked my clients over the years, the same questions that helped me craft their books. I demonstrated how to draft an outline that would make sense to

---

1   Mike is one of only a handful of authors for whom I've written who is open about our collaboration and allows me to talk about it. I love that about him, and that's one of the reasons I still write with him. If you're wondering about my other ghostwriting clients and the books I wrote for them, I'm afraid you'll have to keep wondering, because nondisclosure agreements prevent me from sharing that information publicly.

readers. I explained the concept of delivering on a promise, not just making one.

One by one, the authors' ideas took shape. One by one, they gained confidence in their message as they refined it. One by one, they sat taller in their seats, the way forward visible and their aims affirmed.

I started to see that these people really did want to write a book that changes lives. They weren't interested in a "better business card." I should have expected this, since Mike and Michael subscribe to a much higher standard. Still, it was a welcome surprise. I started to have hope that maybe, just maybe, aspiring authors wanted to give more to their readers, to do better. I knew some of my clients wanted that, but up until then, I thought most people just wanted a quick turnaround, a template, a fill-in-the-blank book that would make all their dreams come true.

Turns out, I underestimated "most people."

That's when I started to think, *Huh. Maybe I* can *teach this.*

Then I had a bigger thought, a bolder thought: *Maybe I can help change the way people think about writing personal and professional development books. Maybe I can inspire authors to want more, to adopt higher standards. Maybe we can get better books published, books that could change the world.*

On the drive back from Maryland to New York, Mike at the wheel, I sat in the backseat and started breaking down the reader-focused framework and methods I'd developed over the years.

To make sure my process worked, I took on new clients: entrepreneurs and speakers who wanted to write the kind of books I once wrote. Instead of ghostwriting their books, I showed them how they could do it and to a higher standard than they believed possible for themselves. From soup to nuts, I guided them through the process from idea to publication, taking notes about my process along the way. With those notes I created a curriculum for an online workshop.

And I declared a new mission: To empower authors with the knowledge, strategies, tools, and support they need to write and publish game-changing books that are in service of the reader.

Then, in 2018, I launched Top Three Book Workshop, a fourteen-week live online class I now hold twice a year for fifteen authors. I call it Top Three to attract aspiring and established authors who want their book to be on someone's top three list of favorite books. Authors who hope to write something that truly changes lives. Authors who are willing to put in the work to create something remarkable. Over the years, this class has grown into a powerful author collective that is among the greatest joys of my life. By providing them with the framework and the feedback they need to craft a book, and by expecting excellence, I found my people at last. They had been looking for a resource to help them write a better book, the book they needed once upon a time, the book they know so many people need now.

Maybe that's why you're here. Maybe you, too, have been turned off by the "better business card" mentality and the book-in-a-weekend programs. Maybe you need a home for your big, bold mission. Maybe you want to write a must-read, and you simply need guidance. I hope so, because that's what you'll find in these pages. This book is not a page-turner; it's a workshop. Writing is my calling, editing is my super-power, and, as it turns out, teaching is my jam. I love it.

I wrote this book because I want you to have access to the frame-works and guidance I once gave my clients and now give my authors in Top Three Book Workshop. Whether you bought it, borrowed it, or checked it out from your local library (yay!), I want you to learn how to write the book that's been on your heart; the book you've been meaning to start, or finish; the book you've been called to write. I don't want you to have to settle for a template or rush to publish. Your ideas, your message, your story deserve more than that. Your readers deserve more than that. They deserve not just your words, but your *craft*. To craft is to produce with care, skill, or ingenuity. In these pages, I can help you develop the skills, and I've got ingenuity on lock. The care, well, that's up to you.

Your book is forever. Let's craft a good one together.

A Note for Authors of Fiction
(This book is not for you.)

THANK YOU FOR your interest in *Write a Must-Read*. This book is for authors and aspiring authors who want to write a must-read transformational book. The methods and frameworks I teach in this book are not meant for authors of fiction.

As an editor of both nonfiction and fiction books, I want to acknowledge that, yes, novels can be transformational. As a child, *Little Women* by Louisa May Alcott illuminated a path for me, a path I am still on to this day. As a teenager, I lost myself in Louise Erdrich's books, especially *Love Medicine*, which taught me the kind of writer I want to be and is still on my list of top three books I'd take to a desert island. And as an adult, *The Four-Gated City* by Doris Lessing changed my perspective about my family and helped me heal old wounds.

All that said, you will not find answers about how to write a must-read novel in these pages. I wrote this book for people who want to write a prescriptive nonfiction book designed to help the reader get what they want, to make something better, to find new ways to live and work.

However, a few chapters could be helpful to you.

- If you're plagued by self-doubt and struggle to get past "writer's block," read Part Two: Draft, Chapters 7 and 8. I developed a system for finishing a first draft that works (almost) every time, and it will (likely) work for you.

- You may also find Part Three: Edit useful, especially if you wonder how you'll know you're done with your manuscript and ready to submit to an agent or editor. I created a Must-Read Editing Method that can be adapted for fiction that breaks the process down into manageable chunks. Read Chapter 9 and Chapter 12, for sure; you may also find useful bits in Chapters 10 and 11.

- Although I've never tried this with a novel, my Feedback Protocol for Ideal Readers may help you as well. If you try it, let me know how it goes. That's in Chapter 14.

- And finally, Chapter 15 is a crash course in publishing, and I hope you read it. If you don't want to buy this book just for that chapter, you can download it for free from my website (ajharper.com).

If you do use my Reader First method or any other frameworks or ideas in this book for your fiction, please let me know. I'd love to hear from you.

Happy writing!

Reader First,
Last, and Always

IT WAS THE fastest I ever spent $1,500. It was also the only time I booked a trip without first consulting my calendar—and checking with my wife.

The subject line caught my eye: "Spend the Day with Steven Pressfield."

I opened the message immediately. Now, you should know that I hate email, and because I am usually writing or editing, I have a bad habit of letting emails pile up, unanswered. Promo emails? Forget about it. I am an email marketer's worst nightmare—I almost never open them.

So, why did I click on the email about spending the day with Steven Pressfield?

Because his book *The War of Art* changed my life.

Pressfield had never done an event like that before, and the prospect of spending a day with him, learning from him in person, was so exciting, I didn't hesitate to open the email. I also didn't hesitate to hit the "buy" button and plunk down a bunch of money for the one-day experience. I didn't care what it cost. Okay, I cared. I just didn't care enough to hesitate.

Within two minutes of receiving the email, I registered as one of the lucky thirty-five. Within ten minutes, I booked my flight to Nashville where the event would be held. I didn't check first to see if it would take me away from something important. I simply had to see him.

I ended up squeezing the trip in between two other trips and only spent about twenty-six hours in Tennessee. I arrived late the night before with a belly full of butterflies. From the time I left New York, I tried to think of something appropriate to say to Mr. Pressfield. However much I enjoy someone's work, I'm not the type of person who waits at stage doors or stands in line to get autographs. I cringe from second-hand embarrassment whenever people try to talk to celebrities. Still, this was my chance. I'd have to come up with something.

Because we were a small group, I expected to be among strangers. Which is why I was so surprised to spot my friend Susan Michal sitting in the front row. If not for her beckoning me over to sit next to her, I probably would have found my "usual" seat in the back row, chair closest to the door.

When Mr. Pressfield arrived, the butterflies in my belly multiplied by ten. Is this how people feel about meeting boy bands? Or sports heroes? Because, wow.

A tall, soft-spoken man with a kind face, he shared his thoughts on the artist's journey and stories from his early life as a writer. Every so often he referred to his loose, typewritten pages, which he left on the table just inches from my own notebook. As he spoke, I took copious notes. One of his comments about Joseph Campbell's breakdown of the Hero's Journey had me buzzing in my seat, looking around the room to see if anyone else noticed the story structure glitter bomb he had just dropped. (More on that later.)

At the break, Mr. Pressfield remained in the room, scanning his papers just a foot away from me. While I tried to muster the courage to get his attention, the woman at the table next to mine motioned him over and said, "Your book changed my life."

She clutched her copy of *The War of Art* to her chest and then slowly slid it across the table toward him. I was close enough to see the deep creases along the spine from years of reading and rereading.

She opened the book and proudly displayed marked-up pages. She had underlined, circled, and highlighted passage after passage. So many corners had been turned down, the book had expanded in size, as if someone had dipped it in water and left it in the sun to dry.

"You probably hear that all the time," she said.

Mr. Pressfield offered an unassuming smile and nodded. "A fair amount, yes."

I kicked myself for forgetting my own copy of *The War of Art*. Not because I wanted an autograph; I, too, wanted to show him my well-loved book, evidence that it had made a difference in my life. A visual representation of how much it meant to me, how much it *still* means to me. I'd lost count of how many times I'd read it.

Tell him your story, I thought. *Tell him why you're here.* I tried to find the words to say it succinctly, not to take up too much of his time.

After he autographed the woman's copy of his book, I seized the moment.

"I quit my job because of that book," I blurted. Not exactly eloquent, but okay.

His eyes narrowed. "How did that turn out for you?"

"Very well. It was one of the best decisions I've ever made."

His shoulders relaxed and he smiled again. "Good. People tell me that often, and I'm always afraid they went broke."

Yes, *The War of Art* inspired me to quit my job. Steven Pressfield didn't tell me to do it; I finally summoned the will to do it, because of his words. After reading his book, I won my decades-long battle with writer's block and devised a system, which I share later in this book, to ensure that it would never happen again. I also vowed that I would never take a "straight" job again—the day jobs many artists take to support themselves while they write, paint, make music. And I didn't. I read his book in 2004 and by March 2005, I was done with straight jobs forever.

Through his book, Pressfield introduced me to the concept of Resistance and, through practice, I was able to develop a system that worked for me. It worked so well, in fact, I stopped believing that writer's block was a thing—because it isn't. That was the missing piece I needed to follow my heart, to follow my dreams. If it weren't for his book, I'm quite certain I would not be living the life I live today, the life I love. And you would not be reading *this* book, because it would not exist.

I did get in trouble with my wife for booking the trip, by the way, because I had forgotten that she had purchased tickets for us to see Brandi Carlile at Madison Square Garden for a special date night. That did not go over well. At all. She forgave me, but I'm pretty sure she's still mad about it. Was seeing Steven Pressfield worth the expense and the argument with my wife? Yes, it was. To have the chance to meet and learn from someone who changed the course of my life was worth that and more.

When you write a book that helps a reader transform some aspect of their life, they become your ardent follower, your raving fan, your ambassador. They don't hesitate to take you up on your offers. They sign up for your classes. They buy your next book, and your next book, and your next—often without thinking about it. They move heaven and earth to gain access to you. And they help you sell your book. I have recommended *The War of Art* to hundreds of students, clients, colleagues, and friends. I have purchased dozens of copies to give to people. Heck, I'm telling you how awesome it is right now, which will probably lead to more book sales for Steven Pressfield.

All that is possible when you set out to write a must-read.

Think about the books that changed your life. The books you will never part with, that survive through various moves and stages of your life. The books you underline, dog-ear, and highlight. The books you keep on your nightstand, because you want to read them over and over. The books you may not read again but keep as a souvenir for the experience you had reading them, or to remember all that you accomplished because you read them. These are the books you give as gifts and recommend to people. These are the books you buy in paperback, ebook, and audiobook because you want access to all the versions on all your devices. These are the must-read books that make it onto your top three list of faves.

Imagine writing a book that inspires change in readers, that motivates them to fix something, change their mind about something, or change their behavior, to grow, to make bold decisions and take important action. Imagine writing a book that readers underline, dog-ear, and highlight; a book people reread again and again and again. Imagine writing a book that people love so much, they fly across the country just to meet you and say, "Thank you. Your book changed my life."

This is the book you are about to learn how to write.

The Reader Transformation Sequence

You have big dreams. You want to make an impact—on your industry, your community, your country, the world. You want to change things for the better. Show people the way, a better way. You want to become an industry leader, or start a movement, or grow your brand exponentially. To do this, you're going to have to sell a lot of books. A whole lot. And to sell a lot of books, you're going to have to get a lot of people to tell other people your book is a "must-read." A lot, a lot.

To sell books, many authors shift their focus from writing to book marketing and the launch. This is a very important part of authorship and I hope you give your book the push it deserves. The problem is, when we focus solely on the launch, we start to think primarily about getting people to buy our book, and not much beyond that. This is one reason so many people end up with short-lived "bestsellers" that no one can remember a few months later.

Your book becoming a bestseller is not a fixed state. Most—and I do mean most—of the Amazon "bestsellers" made it to the top of an obscure category for a day or so, and then nothing. Even some *New York Times* bestsellers don't sell well past the first week. Why not? Why doesn't bestseller status lead to more book sales for some authors?

The answer is simple. Few buyers actually read the books they purchase, and fewer still finish them, and almost no one is actually better because they read them.

If you buy a book but don't read it, what's the likelihood that you'll tell someone else to buy it? Or if you buy it and read part of it? Or if you buy it and read most of it, but don't actually follow the author's advice?

When a book languishes in your "to be read" or "to be finished" pile, it's not top of mind when someone asks you, "Read any good books lately?" So a book that sells well right out of the gate can easily fizzle out because no one is recommending it.

What you want is a perennial bestseller, a book that sells well year in and year out. That's a book that will change *your* life. And to get that book, you need to first be mindful of what I call the Reader Transformation Sequence: buy, read, finish, act on, tell. You want readers to buy your book, read it, finish it, act on your advice, and then, because some aspect of their life has been transformed, tell someone about it. Or tell a lot of people about it. A lot, a lot.

How do you do that? Here's a quick reference I hope you'll jot down and keep close as you read this book:

Buy. Readers will buy your book because you have a solution for their problem.

Read. Readers will read your book because you see them and you get them.

Finish. Readers will finish your book because they trust you.

Act on. Readers will follow the advice in your book because you believe in them.

Tell. Readers will tell people about your book because *they* believe in *you.*

You've probably heard that you need to write a book that is a solution to your reader's problem. That's usually where most people stop thinking about the reader. And this is why so many books fail to catch on. You've got to think about your reader beyond getting them to buy the book. If they don't see themselves on the first page, it's not likely they will actually read your book. Maybe they'll finish the first chapter, but if you don't connect with them, they will set your book aside. If they do feel seen by you, you can still lose them at any time if they think you're full of it, if you don't have the solution to their problem or don't understand their perspective, or if you ask too much of them. This is when you lose their trust, and it's nearly impossible to get back.

If they do trust you, they'll finish your book. Still, it's tough to get them to act on your advice. People are busy. Most won't do the thing you ask them to do, which could mean they won't experience the transformation you promise. But when they know you believe in them, when you've made it easy for them to take action and inspired them to try, most of your readers will do the thing. And when all of that happens—when they buy, read, and finish your book, when they act on your advice—a magical thing happens. Now they believe in you. And when they believe in you, they tell the world.

So, how do you pull off this Reader Transformation Sequence? How do you do this when you aren't even sure your idea is book-worthy? When you aren't sure anyone will want to read what you have to say? When you're concerned you don't have what it takes to write something readable, much less remarkable?

Focus on your reader.

To get them to read, finish, act on, and finally tell someone about your book, start with your reader and stay with them all the way through.

The Key Understanding That Will Make Any Book Better

Have you ever read a book that felt like listening to a college lecture? Or your blowhard cousin who tells everyone what to do? Or a guru who thinks the circumstances of your life don't matter? A long pitch from a smarmy salesperson? A conversation with a party guest who goes on and on about themselves and never asks you anything about yourself? Or a frustrating exchange with a tech support person who thinks you're clueless? All those books have the same problem: somewhere along the way, the author forgot about their reader.

To write a transformational book, the key point you need to understand is that a book is not about something. A book is *for* someone. It's not about your topic; it's for the people you serve and the people you hope to serve.

When authors write books about something, they may have a reader in mind and they may want to be of service, but their focus is on their collection of knowledge and stories: What is my reader demographic? What is my message? How much of my knowledge should I share? What stories do I want to include? How long (or short) should my book be? Should I include action steps? How should I organize my book? How can I get on the bestseller list? It's not that they don't want to write a great book; it's just that they are focused on themselves. My book. My knowledge. My stories. My success.

When authors write a book *for* someone, they are focused solely on that person—their Ideal Reader. Now the questions change. Who is my reader (and what do they want, fear, struggle with, wonder about)? Which message will help my reader change (get what they want)? What can I promise my reader? What do they have to understand and what actions do they need to take for me to deliver on that Promise? How can I help them better understand my teaching points? How can I help them feel better about themselves? Where do I need to simplify my process so they can take action? How do I want them to feel at the end of my book? How can I engage with and continue to serve my readership after the book comes out?

When the focus changes, the book changes. Instead of a decent collection of your thoughts, ideas, and stories, you now have a book that is designed to provide the reader with a life-changing experience. We can give the reader our best stuff and hope they take it and run with it, or we can intentionally craft a book that is transformational in and of itself, so that the reader changes by the time they turn the last page. Which book do you think people would treasure? Which book do you think people would tell their friends about? Which book do you want to write?

A must-read book . . .

1 Connects with the reader where they are.
2 Respects the Reader Journey.
3 Delivers the promised transformation to the reader.

Notice that your reader factors in all three of these fundamentals.

A book is not about something. A book is *for* someone. This is the foundation of everything I write, everything I edit, and everything I teach. Making this simple shift will automatically help you write a better book. Even if you stop reading this book right now, you can up your game by keeping that philosophy firmly in mind.

To help my student authors remember this, I coined the phrase, "Reader first, last, and always!" We've shortened it to "Reader First." Write it down. Post it on your computer. Type it at the top of your blank document before you sit down to write.

You may have come across the phrase "serve your reader." You may also have been given the advice to write a book that changes lives. This is not a new concept. The challenge is that these ideas are almost always limited to the ideation stage of book development. So, for example, you might consider these points when you're trying to figure out which of your book ideas would best serve your Ideal Reader and which message would help them most. That's usually where "serve your reader" and "change readers' lives" ends—in the beginning.

To truly serve your reader and have any hope of actually changing their life with your book, you have to do more than ask yourself that question. You must hold them the whole way through. You have to put the reader first, last, and always. This means from idea through execution. From writing the super-rough draft of your book all the way through engaging with readers after it's published. Reader First is not just an idea; it's a craft.

The beauty of putting your reader first is, you will always have an answer. When you wonder, "Should I tell this story?" you simply have to ask yourself, "Does this story serve my reader?" When you aren't sure what content you'll need for your book, you simply ask yourself, "What do I need to include that will help me deliver on my Promise to my reader?" When you wonder how long your book should be, or if it should have action steps, or if you need illustrations, or a companion workbook, or, or, or... the answer is always, "Would this serve my reader?"

And, because you will always have an answer, you are less likely to give up on your book and stick it in the proverbial drawer. Reader

First can save you from that fate. When you get stuck, when you don't think you can go on, when you are convinced that no one will want to read your book, when you believe the nasty critics in your mind—or in your life—who tell that you're not good enough, talented enough, smart enough, or strong enough to pull this off, Reader First will pull you out of that hole and get you back on track. Because, you see, when we are in service to our reader, helping them is our only goal. We can set aside our desire to be the best, to be perfect, to sell the most books. That ego stuff gets you in trouble. It kills the dream.

We don't need more books that no one reads, that few finish, and still fewer actually follow. We need books that connect with readers, respect their journey, and deliver the promised transformation. You can pull this off. I'm sure of it. And to do that, there's one more shift you'll need to make, one more truth you'll have to accept: writing a must-read book will take much longer than you imagine.

Take the Time to Write a Good Book

I like to declare myself queen of random things. "Queen of Interviews," "Queen of Hallmark Christmas Movies," and the one I say most often, "Queen of Managing Expectations." I keep my expectations low. Like, sub-basement low. Magical underworld low. Scientists believe this is the key to happiness, and it certainly has been the key to mine. The reason I take managing author expectations so seriously, though, is because I've seen too many good ideas die before they became books—and too many great books go unread once they're published.

The dream of authorship is both powerful and precious, and yet in their search for guidance on to how to go about it, many aspiring authors end up settling for easy and fast. Certainly, many people do actually want easy and fast. They want to "get a book done" for a specific event or season, to give away to clients, or just to say they have one. They aren't really interested in people actually reading it. No judgment on those people; they're just not my people.

Sometimes I wonder why so many book coaches and programs tout speed as a benefit of working with them. I don't have the answer, but

I suspect it is in part due to a belief that you can't teach people how to be great writers, so why not make the process easy and fast? From a business standpoint, I guess that makes sense. The problem—the really big problem—is that that approach also breaks hearts.

Yes, you can write the first draft of a book in a few weeks or months. You may even be able to write the first draft of a short book in a weekend—and by short, I mean you can write a pamphlet in a weekend. What you *can't* do is write a great book in a weekend, or in six weeks, or even in three months. This is where the heartbreak happens. Many book coaches and programs lead you to believe that, once you finish your first draft, you can move right into production and publish in weeks, if not days. In production, a copy editor dots your i's and crosses your t's. They fix the grammar, punctuation, and if you're lucky enough to get a *real* copy editor, they'll also fix passive voice and other pesky writing habits newbie authors often have. What they won't fix, however—what they can't fix—are the big issues:

- Does your book speak to your Ideal Reader? Can they see themselves on its pages?

- Does your book meet the reader where they are and take them where they want to go?

- Does your book help them on their journey through your content?

- Does your book deliver on its Promise?

  Beyond serving the reader, there are other concerns:

- Are you writing the book that will help you realize *your* dreams? Is this the right book for your short- and long-term goals?

- Does your book represent all that you are and all that you stand for? Does it sound like you?

- Does your book plant seeds for revenue and reader engagement?

It's damn near impossible to answer these questions without guidance, especially if you didn't even know to ask them in the first place.

Not everyone has the talent of a great writer, but that doesn't mean you can't write a must-read. Still, writing a book is hard. Period. It takes time. A lot of time. The process will challenge you and change you. And that's a good thing.

You may not be able to write a must-read book in ninety days, but I'm 100 percent confident you can write a must-read book—eventually. This book will give you the guidance you need to answer the big questions, a framework to help you outline and draft your book, and an editing system to make sure it all works. You'll also need patience. A lot of it. Will you need help along the way? Absolutely. Publishing is a collaboration, and you need good people. That said, with the help of this book, you can do a lot of the heavy lifting on your own.

Why Not You?

At the Steven Pressfield event in Nashville, I forced myself to line up to get a picture with him. I wouldn't have done it, except my writing partner, Mike Michalowicz, had texted me earlier: "Have an AMAZE-BALLS time with Steven Pressfield. Get pictures!"

Mike knew I would probably skip that part, and he also knew how special this moment was for me.

I did get the picture with Mr. Pressfield, and, in my Minnesota-raised self-effacing way, said thank you for a lovely day. It was a pretty good pic, actually. I really do look like I'm glowing with happiness.

Later that day, while waiting for my flight back to New York, I texted the pic to Mike. I thought about how many times I've seen him take pictures with readers, and my mind wandered to some of my own experiences with them. It's rare for a ghostwriter to be on the receiving end of a reader's adoration. When I was a full-time ghost, I operated my business like Fort Knox. I never told anyone who I wrote for, even if that author had not asked me to sign a nondisclosure agreement (NDA). At times, I had to bite my tongue because someone was talking about a book they read, which I wrote. Mike, though, had decided to be open about our writing partnership. He's a bit of a rock star, and sometimes, despite my best efforts to hug that wall at the back of the room, his fans find me.

Once I was at a networking event, meeting my obligatory five new people, when someone I introduced myself to read my name tag, put two and two together, and then did the "We're not worthy" bow from *Wayne's World*. I'm always a little uncomfortable in those situations because really, Mike's books are Mike's books, not mine.

At another event, a speaker called me up on stage in front of hundreds of people and told everyone that I write with Mike. I did not expect that! You've never seen me move to the back of the room so fast, I assure you. I managed to slip out before anyone could stop me, made it all the way to the elevators, and pressed the button for my floor. Then, like in the movies, someone slid their hand in between the doors just as they were about to close.

Suddenly I was alone in an elevator with a young woman with big eyes. She wore her hair in a high ponytail and pulled a rolling suitcase behind her.

"I'm sorry to bother you," she said. "Is it true you wrote *Profit First* with Mike?"

I nodded and glanced at the control panel. Nine floors to go.

"Could you tell him something for me? I know it's a lot to ask, and you don't know me, but I may never get a chance to tell him myself."

I softened and offered a smile. "Of course. I'm happy to do that."

"Could you . . ." She adjusted the strap on her backpack, glanced at the ads on the wall, and then looked me straight in the eyes. "Could you tell him his book saved my business? We were . . . we weren't going to make it. We almost lost everything. Then I found his book and we turned it around."

This woman wasn't a "fan." She didn't want a piece of Mike. It wasn't about an autograph or a picture or a claim to fame. She was a reader who wanted to thank him, because his book changed her life. And if she couldn't do it directly, she would do it through me. As simple as that.

Oh, man. So this is what it feels like.

"Yes. I will tell him," I said.

The doors opened for my floor, she thanked me, and we said our goodbyes. Before I even made it to my room, I'd passed the woman's message along to Mike and added, "It means a lot to me to see first-hand how we've changed readers' lives."

Now, sitting at the Nashville airport, having just met *my* literary hero, I thought about my authors—the students and clients who trusted me with their book babies. *This is what I want for them*, I thought. I want their readers to seek them out. To write them about their progress. To wait in line to meet them. To stop them in elevators and say, "Thank you so much."

This is what I want for *you*, lovely reader.

And before you think, "Who am I to think so big?" or some version of that nonsense, let me tell you that "AMAZE-BALLS" Mike, rock star Mike, well, he had just as much experience as you, once upon a time. When I met him, he was unknown and super green. He didn't even call himself an author. He didn't know how to put his reader first, how to tell a great story, or how to deliver real change on the page. He hadn't developed his voice or his vision. He simply wanted to make a difference for entrepreneurs and to write an excellent book that would be a game-changer for them.

He learned. He got better. He focused on craft.

He devoted himself to authorship. And he became an author.

You can, too.

If you have big dreams for your book, don't ask yourself, "Who am I?"

Ask a different question.

"Why *not* me?"

PART ONE

Develop

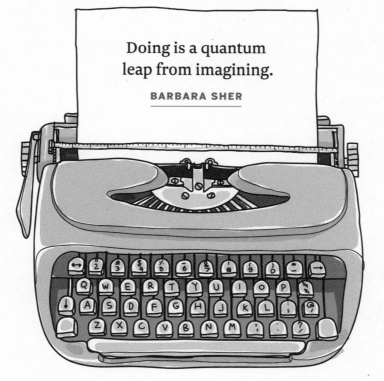

Doing is a quantum
leap from imagining.

BARBARA SHER

Connect with Your
Ideal Reader

YOUR READER WANTS your book to be the one. The book that will make their dreams come true. The book they've been waiting for, searching for; the book they hope exists but fear may be just a myth. The last book they'll need to read on the topic, the one that will transform them once and for all.

If you think this sounds like a romance novel, that's intentional on my part. Much like dating, your reader tries out books on your topic looking for the perfect match—the book that finally, finally helps them get what they want. Sure, some of your readers aren't that serious about it. Maybe they read a hundred books a year and yours is one of that bunch. Maybe they're simply looking for a few golden nuggets and then they'll move on to the next book. For the most part, though, readers come to your book with the hope that it will help them get closer to the life they imagine for themselves.

Avid readers are like serial daters. They've had a lot of bad blind dates—with books. Because some of them have read a lot of books on your topic, those readers come to yours with a mixture of hope and skepticism. Andrea Lee, coaching pioneer and author of *We Need to Talk*, refers to it as having "one foot on the gas and one foot on the brake." To deliver, to ensure your book will be *the one*, you have to get your reader to keep their foot on the gas. You want them to keep reading your book, keep moving forward, keep doing all the things you know will help them solve their problem and get what they want. The first step in doing that is to connect with them where they are, and to do that, you have to get to know them. Very, very well.

Your book can't be all things to all people, but it can be the perfect match for *your* people. This is the foundation of everything I teach. In Chapter 1, you learned that a book is not about something, it's *for* someone. In this chapter, you'll get up close and personal with your reader so you can write a book that delivers for them.

You See Them and You Get Them

Have you ever called in sick to finish reading a book? I have. Only once, but I'll never forget that day. I had been reading Wally Lamb's debut novel, *She's Come Undone,* and I legit could not put it down. It's a coming-of-age story about a young girl who uses food to process her emotions and her journey into adulthood as an obese person. I'm not doing the book justice with that summary. The honesty hooked me and her hope kept me turning the page. Throughout my day, thoughts about how to get back to that book distracted me from nearly every task.

One morning I woke up, glanced at the book on my nightstand and thought, *I have to finish this today.*

I spent the entire day reading, most of it in the bathtub. My room-mates were shocked that I had called in sick so that I could read a novel, especially because I hardly ever called in. I'm from the Midwest—we joke that we'd only call in sick if we were dead. Too loud to ignore, the call of that story won out over my values.

Never before had I felt so *seen* when reading a book. From page one, I kept thinking, *Did Wally Lamb read my journals? How does he know this stuff about me?* Have you ever felt that way? That a book was written with you in mind? That an author can see inside your heart?

I don't know that I would identify with *She's Come Undone* at this stage in my life. Probably not. That said, I haven't parted with my waterlogged copy in the more than twenty years since I read it. I've carried it with me through six moves, packing and unpacking it, packing and unpacking it again and again. Every time I look at it, I smile, because it was so influential in my life at the time. It made me feel seen and heard, and hopeful about my future. That's what a book can do for a person. That's what *your* book can do for your readers.

For me and for most authors, there's no higher praise from a reader than "I couldn't put it down." In fiction, a well-drawn protagonist and well-constructed narrative can inspire that commitment to a book. In nonfiction, your voice, message, and Promise to the reader do the same. But to compel a person to set the world aside so they can finish your book is next level. To do that, you'll have to create a connection with your reader on page one and hold it all the way through. That connection is possible when they feel that you see them and you get them.

Everyone wants to feel seen. This is a basic and powerful human desire, and yet many people would say they don't feel seen. It's a painful feeling, isn't it? To feel as though no one listens or understands. To want people to notice your struggle and frustrations and to acknowledge how hard you're working to get this thing you want or need.

Imagine if you opened a book and actually saw yourself on the very first page? You would feel an instant connection to the author. The connection between you and your reader is only possible when you have clarity about who they are, what they want, and what they think stands in their way.

Classics Are Reader-Driven

The most compelling fictional stories—novels, plays, movies—are character-driven, which means the characters move the story forward. The novels, plays, and movies we don't love as much are very often plot-driven, meaning someone comes up with a concept and plugs characters into that scenario. I'm sure you can come up with exceptions to my opinion; there are always exceptions. Still, I believe that in the stories that grab us and endure, in the stories that become classics, the characters come first and the plot is rooted in what they want and the internal and external obstacles in their way.

My dad loves the classic film *Casablanca*, set during World War II, so I've seen it approximately two hundred times. The main character, Rick, is an American expatriate who owns a nightclub in Morocco. The love of his life, Ilsa, walks into the club with her husband, a leader in the anti-Nazi Resistance. She soon reveals she never stopped loving Rick. Everything that happens next is driven by what Rick wants and what Ilsa wants, and all that stands in their way. They are both dealing with external obstacles—the inability to get out of Casablanca and, hello, Nazis. And they are both dealing with internal obstacles—torn between their love for each other and doing what they feel is the right thing. Every twist and turn connects to what they want and why they may not be able to get it.

Just as character drives story in fiction, when you put your reader first, they drive every component of your book: the stories you tell (or don't tell), the information you share (or don't share), the exercises you offer (or don't offer), and the research you use (or don't use). You'll see how Reader First is enormously helpful in just about every aspect of writing and editing your manuscript.

You're not writing just any book. You're writing a book with the intention that it will become a classic. That's why your book is not about something; your book is *for* someone. So, who is your Ideal Reader?

Who Do You Want to Hang Out with for the Next Few Years?

When I was a full-time ghostwriter, total strangers would call me because they "got my number from so-and-so." I imagined my clients sitting at a corner booth in a dimly lit hotel bar, sliding my number face-down across the table to the friend they just met at this or that conference. Reality was probably pretty close to my fantasy. Since I didn't market myself, you had to know someone to find me. So when people called, I assumed they were vetted by my peeps. That was not always the case.

Sometimes the person on the other end of the line asked for something ridiculous. I'd end up in a long conversation, listening to what they wanted (an awesome book, in their voice), their ideas for their books (me, me, me), what type of outcome they wanted for their book (bestseller!). I always saved my "What's your timeline?" question for *after* I listened to their wants and needs. That's usually when I had to drop the ball that getting what they wanted would take about four times as long as they planned. Most of the time, well, let's just say that revelation was not well received.

One morning, I answered the phone while scrubbing crayon marks off my kitchen floor. I was in no mood for another forty-five-minute conversation with a referral, so after he introduced himself, I asked, "What are you doing for the next few years?"

"What do you mean?" he said.

"What you want, the quality book you want, that requires an investment of years, not months."

"But my colleagues got their books out in less than ninety days."

"From start to finish?" I asked.

"Yes."

"That means they skipped several steps. It also means they have crap distribution. And I'll bet they stopped marketing it after it came out." I sighed and sat down next to my bucket of soapy water. "What you want, it takes years because it takes months to develop and write your book, months to edit it, months to allow enough lead time for proper distribution, and *years* to build readership after your book comes out."

Click.

Yup. He hung up on me. At first I was mad, but then I realized that conversation clocked in at under five minutes, so I'd saved myself a lot of trouble.

After that, I led every conversation with a prospective client with that same question: "What are you doing for the next few years?" Committed authors, even if they were momentarily taken aback by the question, took me seriously and adjusted their plans. Those who just wanted to "get a book out" were quick to end the call. Good.

Think about your Ideal Reader in the context of years, not months. Who do you want to think about for the next six months to a year while you write and edit this book? Who do you want to serve long after the book comes out?

Before you can begin to understand your Ideal Reader, you must figure out if you actually want to cater to them. Are they the people you most want to help? And will helping them help you realize your dreams? Authorship is a big investment of time, and publishing is a long game. Over the months and years, your commitment to your reader will carry you through when you feel like giving up. So, who do you want to hang out with for the next few years?

Your Ideal Reader Is Not Everyone

You've probably heard this before, but when you write for "everyone," you appeal to no one. You may also think your book would appeal to everyone, so how do you reconcile those two truths?

Here's the thing: Writing for everyone is really, really difficult. You might think it's easier to communicate in generalities, but it really isn't. It's ineffective, because unless you're Freddie Mercury (legendary front man of Queen, in case you aren't familiar with the greatest band of all time), or maybe a cult leader, it's pretty hard to connect with tens of thousands of people at the same time.

Here's the other thing: Your book idea might have appeal for (almost) everyone. But to execute on that idea in a way that will resonate with them, you need to write to a specific audience.

And one more thing: When you write effectively to a specific audience, when you succeed at connecting with them, other audiences will read your work. I call these people your Peripheral Audience, folks who find your book through friends, family, or colleagues who *are* your Ideal Readers and can't stop talking about your book. Peripheral Audiences want to read must-reads simply because they are must-reads. They can find value and inspiration in books that are not necessarily meant for them, simply because the book is so damn good. So don't worry about writing to everyone. If you write a remarkable book that connects with your Ideal Readers, "everyone" will find you eventually.

Your Ideal Reader Is Not an Avatar

In video games, an avatar is the player's persona. In marketing, an avatar is a detailed description of your ideal customer, right down to their personality, likes, and dislikes. When I ask my authors to describe their Ideal Reader, they often come back with an avatar. Something like this:

> My reader is a woman in her mid-forties who has a corporate job and a side hustle. She would like to phase out of her job in the next five years. However, two divorces ate up most of her retirement and savings, so she does not have a sizable nest egg. She's accustomed to having the freedom to travel and buy most things when she wants to buy them. She also has two college-bound children she plans to support until they graduate. To maintain her lifestyle after retiring, she'll need to increase revenue from her business by 400 percent. She would never clip coupons but does like saving money. She is a thoughtful friend but doesn't let new people into her social circle. She wants to find love again and perhaps remarry.

That's a lot of detail, right? Some are even more specific, down to the type of breakfast cereal their Ideal Reader eats. If you find the process of creating an avatar useful, by all means, go ahead and do it. That said, I don't recommend it. I've found that authors can get stuck, because their avatars are so detailed that they can't figure out how to write to anyone besides that person. It trips them up. They ask me questions like, "If my avatar eats oatmeal for breakfast, will the donut-lovers feel left out?" Okay, I'm exaggerating a bit, but not much. They do wonder if they will alienate other readers who don't share the same set of circumstances, or like the same things. Should they reference several sets of circumstances to appeal to more people? Should they list a bunch of likes and dislikes? Pretty quickly, they freeze up and stop working on their book, because they've boxed themselves in with the detailed avatar.

Some aspects of creating an avatar are helpful—the psychographics. That's what we focus on in workshop. Here's why: your Ideal

Readers may come from different backgrounds and circumstances (demographics), but their problems, desires, and challenges in pursuit of their desire (psychographics) are the common denominator.

Stop for a moment and take that in. You are not writing for people who have identical lives. You are writing for people who share the same goal—to achieve something, to fix something, to learn something. In most cases, what binds them together is that goal and the obstacles—real or imagined—that stand in their way. Their hearts and minds, not their personalities and buying patterns.

My workshop seems to attract more women than men, and yet I don't market exclusively to women. This book is not written *for women*. This book is written for authors and aspiring authors who want to write a book that changes lives but are struggling with how to pull that off, and who may not realize that they need to shift their focus from themselves to their reader. Could be a person of any gender. Could be someone young, someone in midlife, someone hitting that "wise old sage" phase. Could be a person who has plenty of cash to invest in their dream or someone who works two jobs just to keep food on the table. Introverts. Extroverts. Ambiverts (that's me!). Newbies, experts, and everyone in between. None of that actually matters. Know why? Because what matters most is what you want and what you think stands in your way to getting it.

Of course, as ever, there are exceptions. Sometimes you do need specifics about gender or circumstances. For example, one of my authors, Sally Clark, is writing for stay-at-home moms who used to have thriving careers and miss their old lives. She decided on that specificity because that unique set of circumstances causes the problems that she addresses, and because her solution to that problem is rooted in women gathering to help other women practice self-care. Notice, though, that her demographic is still quite simple. She's not beholden to any other defining characteristics.

Now it's time for you to get clarity about your reader.

What follows is the first of several workshop exercises that will help you craft a must-read, transformational book. It's imperative that you do the exercises in this chapter and the next two (Chapters 2–4). Several of my advance readers noted that doing this work gave them a deeper understanding of the rest of the book, so please don't skip it.

WORKSHOP: CRAFT A READER STATEMENT

FICTION AUTHORS create "character bibles" that are so detailed, they put the marketing avatar to shame. For our purposes, we start building what I call a Reader Profile, which is designed to help you get clarity about your reader, beyond demographics. This is the first homework my authors complete. Download your own copy of the Reader Profile from the Must-Read website (writeamustread.com/tools).

Born of the questions I found most helpful when interviewing ghostwriting clients on our kickoff call, the Reader Profile is the beginning of the process that will ensure you can pull off the Reader Transformation Sequence (buy, read, finish, act on, tell). It informs every other aspect of getting your book out into the world—developing, writing, editing, publishing, and marketing your book. Please, one thousand times please, do not skip this step. Even if you think you know your reader very well, don't skip it.

For now, let's work on part one of the profile, the Reader Statement. To be clear, I want you to complete the entire worksheet, and I'll walk you through that later in this book. But I broke this exercise out for you because I've found that even without the rest of the profile, you can move forward when you have a Reader Statement.

This is a good time to remind you that creative work is a messy process. It's not only okay to tinker with ideas and words; it's encouraged. By me. I'm encouraging you to stay open to kicking things around until you feel solid enough to move forward. I wish I could tell you there is a wrong and right way to do this, because I know that would make life simpler. The thing is, while I can give you guidance, it's your book. And it's your reader.

1. How would you describe your reader? Start with demographics. Are you writing for stay-at-home parents? Retired veterans? Cosplay enthusiasts? Dolly Parton fans? You can be as general (health care practitioners) or as specific (therapists) as you like. Remember, we're just tinkering right now.

I am writing for:

_____

2. As it relates to your topic and/or expertise, what does your reader want? What words would _they_ use to describe it? Financial security? Peace of mind? A better marriage—or a hot date? Do they want to learn how to do something or get better at something? Do they have a long-held dream they want to fulfill? Do they need relief?

My reader wants:

_____

3. How would your reader describe their core problem, that which gets in the way of getting what they want? Again, use your reader's language here. Would they say it's a time management issue? Fear of failing? Are they dealing with a chorus of naysayers? Do they procrastinate too much? Are they too afraid to take the first step because they're worried that they'll be rejected? Do they need more education, money, or connections?

My reader would describe their problem/obstacle as:

_____

4. What do you think prevents them from successfully solving their core problem so they can get what they want? You know things your reader doesn't know. You've been where your reader has yet to go. Sometimes the way your reader describes their problem is exactly right and you would describe it the same way. Often, though, you know that your reader's perception of their core problem isn't really the main thing standing in their way. So, what's really going on? Do they *think* it's a time management issue but you know the main problem is that their identity is tied to work? Would they say their main obstacle is fear of failure, and you know it's really fear of success?

I would describe my reader's problem/obstacle as:

_____

5. Now that you've answered questions 1–4, fill in the blanks to complete the following phrase:

I am writing for _____

(demographic) who want _____

but are struggling with (core problem) _____

and may not realize they are also/really dealing with

_____

    Most of my authors tend to list several things in each fill-in-the-blank field. If you've done that, go back and narrow it down. Your reader may want a lot of things, but what is the outcome they want most? They may have a lot of internal and external obstacles, but what is the one core problem? And, though you may know that there are other issues at play, what is the primary one? If you can't narrow it down to just one answer for each field, limit it to no more than three.

    This exercise could take you twenty minutes or less to complete. If you don't know your reader that well, or if you aren't sure which reader you want to serve, it will take longer, and may require doing some recon.

You'll know you're ready to move forward from this exercise when you can say your Reader Statement out loud and it not only feels right to you, but it's also easy to say and remember. You see, I don't just want you to have the clarity you need to write your book, I want you to have the clarity you need to *talk* about your book. Now. As in, right now. Because when you can say, "I am writing a book for..." opportunities will open for you.

Before you ask, yes, you will likely tweak your Reader Statement. Again, this is a messy process. Even though you may change a word or two later, please jot down your statement on a Post-it and stick it onto your computer. Store it in your phone. Keep it handy wherever you may need to reference it.

As we move through this book, I'll show you how to do whatever I ask you to do. Of course, there are limitations with text and some of you may find it easier to watch me do it. This is why I documented my process in creating this book for you on video, using screen share. You can see me complete each workshop section in my Behind the Book video series, which is free to download from my website (writeamust read.com/behindthebook).

Can You Find Your Reader in Real Life?

Now that you know who your reader is, can you find them? Do you know how to get in front of them? Do you know where they hang out, offline and online? Which meetings, conferences, and events do they attend? What is their primary social media platform? And where else do they show up online? Do they belong to any online groups? Who do they follow? Where do they consume their content and what is their preferred way to consume it? Do they prefer video to text? Do they read the *New York Times* or prefer specific bloggers? Do they listen to podcasts? If so, which ones?

If you're not sure, look to your own preferences. If you're in the same industry or share the same goals or interests as your reader, where do *you* hang out? Which social media platforms do you use? Which events do you attend? Could you find your reader there?

If you can't think of at least five ways to reach your readers, you may need to rework your Reader Profile. It's likely too narrow a demographic. Let's look at this made-up Reader Statement:

> *I am writing for stay-at-home parents of foster children who want to build their self-esteem and sense of safety but struggle with concerns about interfering in the child's relationship with their biological parent, and may not realize they are really worried about losing their own relationship with the child.*

If you were the author of this book, you may find that it's easy to find foster parents and easy to find stay-at-home parents, but not easy to find that subset that identifies as both. Or maybe you can find them, but there aren't that many of them. In this case, you'd need to adjust your Reader Statement to reach a broader audience. You may need to just focus on foster parents, the primary demographic.

These questions are important to consider when you're first getting started because you need to be sure that your Ideal Reader is part of a group large enough to find and sustain sales. And you need to be sure that you can actually reach your Ideal Reader, that there is a pathway to find them, that you can get in front of them easily or with reasonable effort. Can you see at least five ways to get in front of your readers? And does it seem doable? Setting aside any imposter syndrome feelings or thoughts you may be having, do you at least see how you could get your message in front of people where they like to hang out and with people they prefer to listen to?

This early work becomes the foundation of your marketing plan. This book is not specifically about marketing, but we do have to consider cultivating readership when writing our books, and we have to consider how we plan to market and profit from the book. I'll go over how to plant the seeds for revenue and reader engagement in Chapter 13. For now, put your Reader Statement to the test. Is this reader group large enough to sustain sales, and can you reach them in at least five different ways?

WORKSHOP: BUILD YOUR READER PROFILE

DRAWING ON the insights gleaned from the Reader Statement exercise, complete the Reader Profile. If you finished the Reader Statement workshop exercise, questions 1–5, you're already halfway there. If you haven't done this step yet, return to page 33.

1. What do you have in common with your reader, either in the past or now?

_____

_____

2. Answer this question in your reader's voice: "I would be happy if

_____ ."[2]

What do I mean by "in your reader's voice"? Remember, you want your readers to open your book, read the first page, and think, "This book is for me." The best way to do that is to use language they would recognize because they "say it all the time" or because they have those thoughts. So, for this question and all that follow, fill in the blanks as if you are your reader. If your reader represents an earlier version of you, this may be easy for you to do.

3. Answer this question in your reader's voice: "I would be successful if

_____ ."

---

[2] Hat tip to one of my authors, Susan Sandler, who asked this and the following question in her initial interviews for her book. I added these two questions to my existing Reader Profile with her permission.

4. What are your reader's burning questions about your topic? These questions often start with "How can I . . . ?" or "What is the . . . ?" Write the questions in your reader's voice. Try to come up with at least ten.

_____

_____

_____

_____

_____

_____

_____

5. What are your reader's chief concerns about your topic? These questions often start with "I'm afraid I won't be able to . . ." or "I'm worried that . . ." Write the concerns in your reader's voice. Try to come up with at least ten.

_____

_____

_____

_____

_____

_____

_____

6. What is your reader's secret fear, the one they are afraid to admit?

_____

_____

You may find it easy to fill out the Reader Profile. Perhaps you work with clients and hear the same questions and concerns every day. If you know your reader well, you can complete this exercise in thirty minutes or less. If you aren't sure about your reader, if you're trying to decide who you want to write your book for, or if it's been a long time since you were in your reader's shoes, you will need more time.

If you feel unsure about what's going on in your reader's heart and mind, you may need to do some research. Even if you think you've got your reader down, you can learn a lot from seeking answers through surveys and low-key social media posts. One of my clients, Carson Tate, conducted a survey before she started writing her second book, _Own It. Love It. Make It Work.: How to Make Any Job Your Dream Job._ She received thousands of responses and used them to fill out her Reader Profile and complete other book development homework. Because she had thousands of responses, that survey also helped her establish demand for her book, which in turn helped her get a book deal with one of the Big Five publishers. (To learn more about publishing, turn to Chapter 15.)

If you don't want to do an official survey, you could poll the communities in which you know your Ideal Reader hangs out. Or email your list. Start with the first part of the Reader Statement. The "may not realize they also/really" part is a key reveal in your book, so leave that out for now. For example, you might post on social media: "I'm writing a book for so-and-so who want this and that." Then add, "What are your top three questions about this?" In a separate post, ask, "What are your biggest concerns about this?" I suggest splitting up the burning questions and chief concerns into two posts so the answers aren't muddied.

In short, if you're stumped, ask around.

You'll know you're ready to move forward from this exercise when you have specific answers for all the questions.

Your Reader May Be an Earlier Version of You

"This is the book I wish I'd had."

Often, the reader is an earlier version of you. The "before" version. Before you figured out whatever it is you want the reader to figure out. Before you understood the one critical thing that could change everything for them. Before you developed the process that saved your business or your marriage. Before you discovered whatever you want the reader to discover so that they, too, can change their life and get what they want. When you think about what drives your reader, you may find it easier to come up with those burning questions and chief concerns if you consider how you once felt.

You want to help people. Make it easier for them. Show them the way. Lighten their load. Give them a roadmap. The challenge is, as authors we forget what it felt like to be that "before" person and face those obstacles. We forget what it was like to worry all the time. To feel confused, or hopeless, or despondent. Or to carry a set of beliefs that weren't serving us. Or to be stuck in a mindset that was not helpful. We want to show our readers that we are past all that "before" stuff because otherwise, why would they read our book? Why would they listen to someone who hasn't put the past firmly behind them and fulfilled all their dreams, and who has their shit firmly together?

Listen, your reader needs to believe they can get where you are, but they don't need you to be as far ahead of them as you may think. And they don't want to hear from someone who never made a mistake, or feels down, or deals with self-doubt. Readers want realness from you.

Tap into that person you once were. What did you fear most? What was your secret anxiety, the one that kept you up at night? What were you confused about? What was your private hope, the wish you would not utter for fear it would never come true? Think back to a time before you understood what you know now. This is your reader. Some version of your "before" is their "now," and they are looking to you to show them the way.

If your Ideal Reader is not an earlier version of you, it does not mean that you haven't had at least some of their experiences or that you can't relate to them at all. Think back to a time when you were in a similar position, and recall your thoughts and feelings about the issue. You can also show your experience working with people like them, people who have been in their shoes.

I didn't write this book for an earlier version of me, a ghostwriter who was just trying to figure out how to write better books for people who didn't know how to write a book. Would I have loved to have had this book as a resource when I started out in my fourth-floor walk-up apartment in Brooklyn? You bet I would have. I'd still have it today. It would be so marked up with highlights and underlined words, and little stars in the margins next to content that I *really* wanted to remember.

But I wrote this book for you, the author, the person who wants to write a book that truly changes lives. As I wrote it, I kept in mind an early version of my clients and students. When they come to me, they have the same questions and concerns you have:

Who is going to want to read this? Is anyone going to want to read this?

Is my idea any good? Is it book-worthy?

I'm worried that I don't have what it takes to write a book.

I don't know the first thing about writing a book, or organizing content, or publishing.

I'm afraid I'm not a good writer.

I often say writing and publishing a book for the first time is like going to Mars. You don't know what to expect, you don't know the language (of technology, science, or aliens), you don't know what it will take to get there and if you have enough of it, you don't know what you don't know. So it's my job to help you deal with your "you are here" questions and concerns. It's your job to help your readers deal with *their* "you are here" questions and concerns, and you can look for clues in the earlier versions of your clients, customers, audiences, or students.

This archeological soul work is vital because if you are able to articulate the problem *as your reader would describe it* and speak to their world and their deepest desires, they will absolutely keep turning the page. When was the last time you felt truly seen and heard by someone? It's not a common experience, and yet we crave it. When you can tap into your reader's headspace—soul space—you may end up with comments such as, "I felt like the author wrote this book for me." That is a reader for life.

Your Book in the Wild

One of my favorite quotations is "Be bold and mighty forces will come to your aid." It's attributed to the German poet Johann Wolfgang von Goethe. I read it for the first time at nineteen while working at a temp agency in Beverly Hills. My boss had printed it on purple stationery and framed it on her desk. I wrote it down in my little notebook, and that line stayed with me all these years. As it turns out, credit should go to Canadian clergyman and author Basil King, who said, "Go at it boldly, and you'll find unexpected forces closing round you and coming to your aid." Tom-ay-to, tom-ah-to. Either version is damn good. I'd like you to use it for inspiration when you do this thing I'm about to ask you to do.

Now that you've workshopped your reader and you have a clear statement about who they are, tell some of them. That's right, it's time to admit you're writing a book. We have a tendency to keep quiet about this. If you haven't told anyone yet about your work in progress (WIP), you may have very good reasons for that. In my experience, keeping that secret is usually down to two things: not knowing if we'll finish the book and not knowing how to talk about it.

You already know a book is for someone, and now you know who you're writing it for. So that takes care of the second concern.

Why do I want you to tell someone—tell a lot of people, actually? Because "mighty forces will come to your aid." Every time I ask my authors to share that they are working on a book for so-and-so who want such and such but are struggling with this and that, they make connections with all sorts of people who can help them: collaborators, people they can interview for stories or case studies, influencers who serve the same audience, organizations who may be interested, podcast hosts who want to book them, friends who know an agent, and so on. Talking about the book in a Reader First way increases the like-lihood that you will finish writing it. It's not just about you anymore. Your reader now knows about the book, and they need it.

If you announce you're writing a book on social media and include your Reader Statement, please add the tag #WriteAMustRead. That way, I can find it.

Take your book out of the proverbial drawer and let it live.

Onward!

CLAIM YOUR REWARD

Writing a book is hard, especially if you're doing this on your own. You deserve a reward as you make progress. Once you've completed your Reader Profile, go to the Must-Read website (writeamustread .com/rewards) to unlock deleted content from this chapter and other cool and useful stuff. I've created different rewards for each milestone, so keep checking in.

Craft Your Game-Changing Core Message

I F I WERE to tell you right now, "Yes, your message matters," would you believe me? Maybe not. In fact, I'll go so far as to say *probably* not. We haven't met yet, so, fair. I don't know who you are writing for. And you haven't had a chance to run it by me for feedback. Despite this set of circumstances, I'm absolutely certain that your message matters.

Here's why: I believe if you get an idea for a book, someone, somewhere needs it.

If you are 100 percent confident that you have something important to share that people will want to hear, then you are an outlier. After working with hundreds of authors, I know that their most common underlying fear is that no one will care. They have this little voice in their head that tells them:

"Your ideas aren't original or inspired."

"The world doesn't need another book on this subject."

"Better people than you have already written about this. Why bother?"

To shut that voice up, you need a strong Core Message. Not something that "works for now" or "sounds okay." You need a message that makes your Ideal Reader lean in and say, "Tell me more. Tell me everything." You need a message that reveals your visionary self. You need a message that makes you want to write the shit out of your book.

When you don't love your Core Message, it undermines the writing and editing process, and it happens right away—with the outline. Whenever a colleague mentions they are struggling with structure or flow, I know right away that they likely have a Core Message issue. They think they have it down, but they really don't, and that lack of clarity makes outlining an unnecessarily time-consuming and difficult process. And if they have a Core Message issue, I know they likely have a reader issue—they aren't writing *for* someone; they're writing about something. (Fortunately, you already workshopped your Ideal Reader, so you're good to go. If you haven't done that yet, please stop now and do the Reader Profile exercise in Chapter 2. It's the most important exercise in this book.)

When my authors finally land on their Core Message, it's joyful. Seriously. They light up, because they know they've hit on the heart of their book. Suddenly their apprehension is replaced with excitement. Their mind starts to fill with ideas. They become more confident talking about their book, because they can succinctly describe who it's for and the Core Message that reader needs to hear. That nasty voice that told them they shouldn't bother writing their book becomes quieter and easier to ignore.

Most people get stuck on Core Message because they don't understand what it is and why it's important. In this chapter, I'll walk you through what it is, what it isn't, and a few doorways in to help you find yours.

Your message matters simply because it matters to someone, somewhere. This chapter is designed to help you refine it so you can believe that it does.

A Core Message Is...

Simply put, your Core Message is the foundational truth that your entire book is built on. Everything hinges on it—all the teaching points you want to share and all the change you want your reader to make. Core Message aligns quite well with the *Oxford English Dictionary's* definition of "principle": A fundamental truth or proposition that serves as the foundation for a system of belief or behavior or for a chain of reasoning.

When you challenge yourself to articulate the heart of your book in a clear and efficient statement, you gain the confidence you'll need not only to write your book, but to stay the course in all aspects of publishing. In Top Three Book Workshop, I ask my authors to come up with a Core Message that meets the following requirements:

- **Strong.** Speaks to the solution for your Ideal Reader's core problem.

- **Clear.** Can be communicated in one brief sentence. Occasionally two, if setup is required.

- **Transformational.** Is transformational *on its own.*

Strong you can handle because you completed your Reader Profile. Clear you may not *want* to handle, but you absolutely can.

Transformational is the hard one, and it requires more explanation. What we want here is a Core Message that, if your reader hears it, they could begin to make a change—even if they never read your book and even if they never meet you. This may seem counterintuitive. Why would you want to craft a transformational Core Message that does not require the Ideal Reader to learn more? Because if your message is that powerful, you know your book will be a game-changer. And let's be real: if you heard an author say something that totally blew your mind, you'd read their book. So don't worry—they'll read it. They'll find you. They'll want to hear more.

Here's an example of the development of a strong, clear, transformational Core Message from one of the authors who completed my workshop. Mara Yale's youngest child had a stroke diagnosed days after birth, which caused some challenges with their development. Almost immediately Mara found herself swept up in the opinions of experts, shuffling from one specialist appointment to another like a pinball. Many years later, her child thriving and on track, Mara set out to write a book to empower parents to take control of their child's development.

Few were more dedicated to my Reader First method than Mara. She went all in from day one. She showed up to every class, every writing sprint session, every one-on-one with me, prepared to work. Sometimes that meant connecting to class from her car while she waited for her children to finish soccer or hockey practice. From her Reader Profile, she knew that her reader was an earlier version of herself and realized she needed to craft a Core Message that dispelled the myth that parents of children with developmental challenges must abdicate control to experts. If she could get her reader to at least consider that point, they could dramatically change not only outcomes for their child, but the quality of life for their entire family.

Here's what she came up with.

Ideal Reader: "I am writing for parents who want a map of the future but are struggling with feeling overwhelmed due to an early developmental diagnosis in their child."

Core Message: "Parents create the conditions for optimal development."

For her readers, that is a strong and clear statement. It is also transformational on its own, because even if they don't read her book, they can begin to shift their perspective and become more empowered, which is Mara's aim. For parents who want to feel more in control, this is a message that makes them sit up and take notice. She noted that the reaction she often gets from parents is relief. Sometimes we forget that our readers may be looking for validation, comfort, or peace of mind, not just how to do something.

When I asked Mara why her Core Message resonated with readers, she said, "In workshop you teach about defying conventional wisdom, and it was one that was so clearly opposite conventional wisdom, and yet true. Why should these experts that I see for a fraction of an hour every year or two control my family's whole life? It just really resonated with my own experience."

Her ability to share an efficient yet powerful statement about who her book is for and the foundational truth on which she wrote it gave Mara confidence, and she was able to test it in professional spaces. She followed my advice and started talking about her book with colleagues and at speaking engagements, and received positive responses from people eager to read her book and help her get the word out. She posted in our private Facebook group: "The fact that my book has already generated interest from professionals as well as parents gives me confidence to keep going."

Do you see how crafting a powerful Core Message helps you ignore the nasty voices from your inner critic and stay the course?

Another benefit of crafting a strong, clear, transformational message is that you make it easier for people to talk about your book. If you can't give people the gist, what makes you think your readers will be able to do that? You need shareable, referrable, recommendable content, and it starts with the Core Message.

Strong, clear, and transformational. Those are your marching orders, and fortunately, you already have a head start because you know your reader.

Earn the Second Sentence

We're going for brevity here, folks. As I said above, you need a shareable and referrable Core Message, and that means you need to make sure it's memorable and easy to spit out in casual conversation. You do yourself and the success of your book a huge favor by taking the time to get your Core Message down to one short, easy-to-understand and easy-to-say sentence. That is your challenge, and you can do it.

If you need a second sentence, you're going to have to earn it. That's because if I say you have two sentences, you'll use both of them rather than try to simplify it into one. Two sentences may be required to provide context. We need a second sentence when we first have to dispel a myth or defy some sort of conventional wisdom about our topic, expertise, or industry before we can state the solution.

- "Most people think this. You think that."

- "This outdated way of doing things doesn't work. The solution is this other way."

- "A commonly held belief is harmful. Here is the way out of it."

You need two sentences for this type of Core Message: the setup, which gives context for this way of thinking, believing, or doing that you don't agree with; and the foundational truth you want people to think, believe, or do.

When Mike and I sit down to write a book, we adhere to a set of Immutable Laws and Characteristics that we set when we wrote *The Pumpkin Plan*. These are qualities and standards that must be present in his books. I'll share more about that in Chapter 11, but for now just know that a key factor in determining if we move forward with a book idea is whether or not the Core Message is disruptive. Mike's books bust some widely held notion or way of doing things—not for the sake of being disruptive, but because he genuinely believes that the status quo is BS and he has a better, more effective approach. Why bother writing the book, otherwise?

Each of his books has a two-part Core Message with the same construct: That doesn't work. This does. For example, here's the Core Message for *Profit First*.

Setup: "Traditional accounting methods are killing your business."

Solution: "Take your profit first."

Technically, the second sentence is transformational all on its own, but the setup sentence provides context that is really helpful. It's also super disruptive. He pisses a lot of people off with his books, I'm afraid. (He's fine with it, and so am I.) You may discover that simply by thinking about what you disagree with, you can get at that Core Message faster. People often say that there are no new ideas. That may be true, but what distinguishes your message from others is your perspective. And your perspective may be that the conventional solution for your reader's problem is totally wrong.

In the workshop section below, you'll have a chance to think about what pisses you off about your topic, expertise, or industry. For now, just know that you can earn that second sentence if your Core Message would be stronger by providing context.

Everything Hinges on This Foundational Truth

I don't have much in common with John Briggs. He's a straight, deeply religious man who never curses. I'm a bisexual former Catholic who curses way too much. He tortures himself with ridiculous workout challenges. I prefer to dance around my office every hour or so. He's a numbers guy, I'm a word girl. You get the drift.

I adore John, though, and I consider him to be one of the finest men I know. Despite our differences, we share common values. Among them is a desire to be of service. He is a CPA who also owns a microgym, a small fitness facility that focuses on cross-training. Ever see your friends or neighbors push a giant tire around town? They probably belong to a microgym. Although, likely not John's microgym, because he thinks all that tire-rolling is "silly." Oh, John. No need to be so harsh.

John licensed a *Profit First* derivative book for microgym owners. That means Penguin Random House (the publisher) and Mike Michalowicz (the copyright holder/author) authorized John to use up to 10 percent of the original text in his book. Then John joined my workshop so he could learn how to write it. When I reviewed his week one homework in preparation for a one-on-one, I noticed he had jotted down our Core Message for *Profit First*, which you just learned: "Traditional accounting methods are killing your business. Take your profit first." While true, and certainly relevant for John's audience, John needed a transformational statement that would be a game-changer for them. Sure, the *Profit First* message is a game-changer on its own, but was it really the foundational truth for *his* book?

John understood his niche audience very well. He's one of them, and he also serves them as their CPA and adviser. So I asked him a bunch of questions in his one-on-one to get at his Core Message. What did he want them to understand so that they could really make a change? Something everything else he wanted to teach hinged upon?

We kept at it for a bit, and then I asked, "What would be a reason why a microgym owner might not follow the advice to take your profit first?"

"Because they are in it for other reasons. They want to help people get fit, and many microgym owners believe that money shouldn't be their focus. The client should be their focus, and any talk of money is considered distasteful. The word 'profit' in the microgym space is almost a dirty word. They don't think they deserve to think about taking care of their business or themselves financially."

"So, what message could change their lives if that's all they ever heard from you?"

"If they believed that they deserve to be profitable."

Ah, yes. There it is.

Before his readers could accept the Core Message of the original *Profit First*, they had to believe that they deserved profitability. Without that belief, they may not actually take the steps that John planned to detail in his book.

John's Core Message became "You deserve to be profitable." That message spoke directly to the big issue, the big *silent* issue among microgym owners. In that way, his readers can see themselves in the Core Message. They can identify with it immediately. They can also make a change based on that message and that message alone. Even if they don't read John's book, just shifting their belief on the question of profitability would help them improve their bottom line. It might even save their business.

Now, with the Core Message "You deserve to be profitable," John has a book that is all his own. He is writing a book that is not just about applying the Profit First system to a microgym business, but about shedding old beliefs regarding business viability, owner compensation, and profitability. John has the potential to offer his readers an important reset, not just a collection of ideas and how-tos.

That Core Message set him on a different path for his book. It shaped his outline and his teaching points. It opened up ideas for stories that would speak to the pervasive belief that to focus on profit detracted from one's noble purpose. It got to the heart of the matter, the main obstacle, which then allowed him to show his readers the way forward.

WORKSHOP: CRAFT A CORE MESSAGE

RATHER THAN start with a Core Message and then figure out who needs to hear it, start with your Ideal Reader and figure out what foundational truth would help them get what they want. The way to do that is to start with your reader and then ask yourself a bunch of questions. You may end up with similar answers. You may write multiple sentences instead of one or two. You may think that your responses are clunky—they probably are. No worries. You're in the "tinkering" phase of ideation, and the questions are like having multiple doorways in a hallway. One of them will lead to your Core Message, and you'll have a better chance of finding it if you try to open each one.

Start with your reader. Pull out your completed Reader Profile and ask yourself the following questions:

1. Considering the problem as your reader would describe it, what is your solution?

_____

_____

2. If you view your reader's struggle differently than they do, how would you describe the solution to the underlying problem?

_____

_____

3. Looking at their list of burning questions, how would you answer the question you hear most often?

_____

_____

4. From their list of chief concerns, how would you address the one you know bothers them the most?

_____

_____

5. How would you speak to their secret fear?

_____

_____

6. Complete this sentence: My reader could get what they want if they only knew

_____

7. Complete this sentence: My reader could get what they want if they stopped/started (or stopped and then started)

_____

_____

Now focus on you. Remember, your reader is often an earlier version of you, so by shifting your attention to your own story, you may get to the heart of what you want to say. Again, you may come up with similar answers here, but walk through the doorways anyway and answer these questions about your own experience:

1. What fundamental truth helped you change your thinking about your topic?

_____

_____

2. What wisdom helped you change your behavior?

_____

_____

3. What do you wish you had known years before?

_____

_____

4. What understanding helped things finally click for you?

_____

_____

Now use a wider lens. Quite often, my authors find their Core Message in this part of the exercise. They don't realize that they have strong opinions about the "way things are" and how other people share wisdom, and that those strong opinions can be the differentiator they need to stand out in a crowded group of thought leaders. This next set of questions centers on your topic, industry, and/or area of expertise:

1. What belief or conventional wisdom do you disagree with?

_____

_____

2. What standard practice do you wish people would stop doing?

_____

_____

_____

3. What pisses you off about your industry or the way people talk about your topic?

_____

_____

Now, looking at your answers to the questions above, craft your Core Message. Each one of your answers could be the seed of the message. Remember, this is the foundational truth on which your entire book is built. (Just a tiny amount of pressure. Teeny-tiny.)

Allow about an hour to get your first draft of your Core Message. I say "first draft" because rarely do I encounter an author who nails this very important step on the first try. Queen of Managing Expectations here: If you're not practiced at crafting Core Messages, expect this ideation process to take a couple of weeks to get right. Deep breaths. You'll get it. Start playing with ideas. It's okay if you have a long list at first. It's okay if you have too many words, or too many adjectives, or none of them seem right yet. Push on.

You'll know you're ready to move forward when you can check off the following:

- **Strong.** Speaks to the solution for your Ideal Reader's core problem.

- **Clear.** Can be communicated in one to two brief sentences that are easy to repeat and share.

- **Transformational.** Is transformational _on its own._

One more thing: Whenever one of my authors lands on their Core Message, I get goosebumps up my arms. Maybe you'll get a feeling in your gut when you know you've hit on something. Or maybe it's a "tingly" feeling, as one of my authors described it. I didn't add this to the criteria to check off because I've found that it stresses authors out. It stresses them out because they don't trust their gut—or their goosebumps. They second-guess themselves. Did I really feel that? Do I still love my Core Message? Is it really as awesome as I think it is?

Do I want you to keep going until you feel your version of my goose-bumps? Yes, I absolutely do. We are not going for mediocre here. That said, it could be a later iteration that makes you feel all tingly inside. And that's okay. Check off the three criteria above and move on. If your Core Message needs a little somethin' somethin', you'll find it eventually. You may have to get some help and ideate with someone who has experience, but you will find it.

I'm often asked if Core Message can change in the writing process. Absolutely. You may tweak it here or there, refining it further based on insights you've gleaned in the discovery process that is writing your first draft. That's to be expected. Will you start over from scratch? Maybe. It's not that common among the authors I work with, but it does happen. This is messy work and none of it is wasted. What you want is a Core Message that allows you to move forward. While you do want to check off all three points above, it doesn't have to be perfect. Perfect doesn't exist in authorship or publishing.

A Core Message Is Not . . .

Landing on your Core Message is one of the most challenging exercises in this book. Let's tamp down any anxiety you may have by running through a list of common missteps and misunderstandings, so you can move forward with a little more confidence.

A Core Message is not . . .

A slogan, a tagline, or a title. "Just do it" is Nike's marketing slogan. "Craft a book that changes lives—including your own" is the subtitle of this book, which also works as a tagline. With your Core Message, though, you're not looking for pithy or cute, or clever or witty. Thank goodness, right? You're going for a transformational truth. This is good news, because coming up with slogans and taglines can be really hard. People pay marketing experts a lot of cash to help them with this, so exhale and stop trying to sound edgy.

An elevator pitch. If you haven't heard the term "elevator pitch," it's a short, persuasive speech, usually no more than thirty seconds in length. If you didn't push yourself to come up with a clear, strong, transformational Core Message, you might think you need one. Why? Because you would need the lovely adjectives and bold promises of that pitch to help you feel confident about your message. While you may need an elevator pitch to help you get media placement, you don't need it to share your message with readers.

A book summary. When I ask non-students for their Core Message, I usually get something closer to an overview about their book. Whether they stumble through it verbally or send me something in writing, it's usually at least a hundred words that covers all the things. You know, a "kitchen sink" message.

A mission statement. If you're on a mission to change the world in some small or big way, thank you. I've found that the authors who have a higher calling focused on helping others are more apt to finish their books and see the whole publishing process through. That said, your Core Message is not about your mission. It may help you achieve your mission, but your reader doesn't need it to understand the foundational truth your book is built on.

A theme or topic. Some people mistake Core Message for subject matter or focus. Yours must be transformational on its own, so simply stating the theme or topic of your book isn't going to cut it.

A promise. This is where most of the authors I work with start. They'll give me a draft that includes their Promise to the reader, or is entirely Promise. Your Core Message is not about what readers can expect from reading your book, or the wonderful changes they'll experience, or the future self—or business, marriage, or body—they will eventually get if they follow your advice. Your Core Message is the truth that *facilitates* the fulfillment of your Promise. Don't worry. You'll get a chance to focus on Promise in the next chapter.

I don't expect you to remember all of this as you workshop your Core Message. We fall into what is familiar and comfortable for us, and so some of you will write first drafts that are pitches or taglines, or book summaries, or melded with Promise. That's okay. Keep at it.

Your Core Message Can Change *Your* Life, Too

I really thought I might lose Mike Ciavolino. About five weeks into my fourteen-week workshop, he emailed to say he might drop out. I knew he had been struggling, that he didn't feel qualified to write a book for parents of children with special needs. Dad to triplets, two who are on the autism spectrum, Mike didn't believe that alone made him credible. He owns a marketing firm. He's not a medical professional, a researcher, or some other expert. Who was he to write about it?

"I didn't believe that I had anything to say and that even if I did, it had been said before," Mike told me when I interviewed him for this book. "I couldn't believe my own writing."

I remember that his early drafts focused on sharing tips and research but didn't have a lot of stories. His writing read like a guide-book; it lacked his voice, which I had come to know well. Where was Mike in his book?

At the time, he had settled on this Core Message: "You can get over the overwhelming flood of negative emotions and the fear of parenting a special needs child, and take your life back." You can see that his Core Message is affirming and speaks to what Mike's reader wants, but it's not a foundational, transformational truth that provides a solution to the problem. If we worked on this, I knew I had a chance of helping him make progress with his book.

I'm a recovering boss rabbit and I try to let people chart their own course, but I pulled out my inner Lucy from *Charlie Brown* and told him he couldn't leave the workshop. Nope. Not even going to consider it. Then we met to talk through his Core Message again. We focused on his own story and talked about when he felt the same way his readers feel, when he had some of the same burning questions and chief concerns. We talked about when everything changed for him, the key understanding he had to come to, to make that change. What had he realized that allowed him to love his challenging life parenting kids with special needs?

"I had been resenting the loss of my old life before the kids were born, that I had been looking at our life as though their birth had veered us off course," he told me. "One morning, I asked myself, 'What if this *is* the path we're supposed to be on right now?' It was a moment of acceptance that allowed me to shift my perspective from viewing the challenges of parenting special needs kids through the lens of hardship to seeing it as an opportunity to experience joy."

During that call, Mike landed on his new Core Message, which is one of my favorites of all time:

"Having special needs children in your life is not a detour. It's the life you were meant to live. You can do this."

Goosebumps all the way up my arm. (Notice Mike snuck in a third sentence he felt was important for parents to hear. Do I think he needs it? No. But maybe his readers *do* need it, and Mike is the authority on them. *Reader First.*)

When he said his Core Message out loud for the first time in workshop that week, he teared up. Suddenly he had a fire under him and a newfound positivity.

"When I settled on it, a lot changed for me," Mike told me. "I had spent five weeks of our cohort with my head in the sand not doing anything, just paralyzed by fear. When I changed the message and started to embrace it, I knew what I wanted to write about. Slowly, just by showing up, it became clearer."

Mike's book *SuperParent* is a game-changer for readers. The process of writing it has been a game-changer for Mike, and it began with finding his transformational Core Message.

"When I had it, I felt I could authentically own the space, believe it, and illustrate it through the book and teaching points." And stories. I'll add that for him. Because what had been missing from his early writing now poured out of him. As it turns out, he's a remarkable storyteller, and that Core Message gave him permission to share in the ways his readers need. It also helped him talk about his book with media, which landed him an article in *USA Today*. It was so fun to see his Core Message right there in print.

Where Mike once thought he didn't have what it takes to write a book, that his message didn't matter and he wasn't qualified to write it even if it did, he now considers himself an author.

I believe if you get an idea for a book, you have the capability to pull it off. If you are called to write something, if you are given the gift of inspiration, that means it is worth pursuing and you are up for the challenge. This is not just a nice notion that speaks to my generally optimistic nature. This is based on nearly two decades of experience working with authors, from total newbies to beloved thought leaders.

So often, we think what we have to say doesn't matter, or that there are better books out there written by more qualified people. The truth is, what really works for readers, what really inspires them to read on, to take your advice, to do it, is you. *You.* Your experience paired with your insights is a magical combination that no one else can replicate.

Did you catch that? No one else can replicate what you have, because no one else can be you.

Your Book in the Wild

Once you have two or three possible versions of your Core Message, share it with your Ideal Readers. You might send out an email to your list, or post something in a targeted online group or just on your own page. Make sure to share your Reader Statement, then ask them to vote on your Core Message. This is not a scientific approach, but you'll usually get a sense of what works best for your audience.

Stop what you're doing and post about this right now. I want to you have a good sense of which Core Message you'll run with before you move on to the next step. (And don't forget to add the hashtag #WriteAMustRead. I want to see the fruits of your labor.)

Onward!

CLAIM YOUR REWARD

Once you've completed your Core Message, go to the Must-Read website (writeamustread.com/rewards) to unlock more deleted content from this chapter and other cool and useful stuff.

Commit to a Promise
You Can Deliver

THE SPEAKER moved across the stage like a rock star. The audience, now on their feet, buzzed with the energy and the promise of dreams fulfilled. They could have what the speaker has. They could follow the same path. They could rise up from any challenge and succeed.

The speaker was, without a doubt, a master storyteller.

The speaker was also full of it.

I couldn't pass English in high school and I've written dozens of books,[3] they said.

A ghostwriter wrote my book, they didn't say.

You can become a *New York Times*–bestselling author like me, they said.

I paid one hundred thousand dollars to a firm that gamed the system so I could get on the *New York Times* bestseller list, they didn't say.

I can still remember sitting in the front row at the keynote given by a thought leader I cannot name at a conference I cannot reference,

---

3   For all the copy editors out there, I'm leaving the quotation marks off and using gender-neutral pronouns on purpose. I don't want to use the exact wording because I don't want anyone to trace it back to the person I'm talking about.

watching the audience fill out applications to join their latest program. Some of the people who signed up that day had the money to pay the huge fee, and some of them would go deeply into debt to cover it. They had big dreams, and after listening to the rock star speak, they were sure that those dreams could be fulfilled with their help.

Maybe it would work out. Maybe some of them actually *would* achieve all that the speaker promised that day. I'd been in the business long enough to know that most wouldn't. In the best of circumstances, becoming a successful author is a long, sometimes arduous process. Most people fail because they give up. The grind is too hard. Of course this thought leader didn't want to say any of that, or mention the shortcuts they'd taken to achieve their status. How could they get people to buy into their program if the path to authorship seemed too long and too difficult?

As I walked out of the hall that day and took the elevator up to my room, the thought that had been nagging me for months popped up again: *You can't be a part of this. You have to get off this train.* Because I told the truth about the realities of publishing, I had convinced myself it was absolutely fine that I continued to work with people who used hope as a weapon. I was just a cog in the machine, right? As long as I held fast to my own values, as long as I did my very best to serve people, I could hold my head high. Right?

Except.

Except I *was* a cog in the machine, and that meant I was part of the big lie.

It would take another display of audience manipulation for me to finally admit that I had to get out, career be damned. I stopped taking ghostwriting clients and finished out my contracts, with no real plan for the future. I knew I wanted to continue to write with Mike Michalowicz. He's exactly as he presents himself to be, and I know his heart and intention, so I told him I'd write with him exclusively. (He was pretty happy about that turn of events.)

Unlike Mike, many of the authors I had worked with played a game of smoke and mirrors. They taught people how to become millionaires but they were in the middle of a bankruptcy. They showed people how to build effective teams and yet they couldn't stop the infighting with their own. And they helped people become bestselling authors when they couldn't achieve it without a lot of help and a lot of cash—a fact they omitted from their speeches, stories, and marketing materials. Most of them had started out in the self-help industry pure of heart, but somewhere along their journey they lost their way. They weren't horrible people; they had just bought in to their own hype.

The year I decided to get out, I attended an event in Los Angeles and rang up Lucy, a fellow ghostwriter who had worked with some of the same people. She had gotten out the year before and I wanted to hear her perspective, so I invited her for ice cream. (I realize I sound as though we were in the mob. It really wasn't nefarious, or criminal, but it was just as seductive. Or at least that's what I thought after watching *Goodfellas*.)

"When do you think they changed?" she asked.

When *did* they change? I wasn't sure.

I thought about it for a few bites and then said, "Maybe it starts with the bio. You know the new authors, who write their bios as if they have already achieved everything they want? 'Sought-after' and 'thought leader,' and all those adjectives."

Lucy nodded. "So many adjectives and superlatives."

"Yeah, as if they aren't enough," I added. "They make up something, or exaggerate it, because they feel as though they need to be more than they are."

"And then they start to believe it," Lucy said.

I share this story with you because I don't want you to haul out the adjectives and superlatives to feel as though you have something worth saying. You *do* have something worth saying. Right now. Just as you are. And those adjectives and superlatives lead to promising people the moon, without explaining what it actually takes to get there. You may wonder if anyone will buy your book if the reward isn't big enough. They will. How many people buy it has nothing to do with how big your Promise is; it has to do with delivering on that Promise. When authors feel the urge to promise big things, it's often because they question if anyone will care about their message if they don't. They may not realize it, but at the heart of that giant Promise is the fear that they are not worth the investment.

It's not enough to add a "results may vary" asterisk to bold claims. Promising people the moon and leaving out what it actually takes is a lie—a lie by omission. Would the rock star thought leader have sold as many seats in their publishing program if they explained that they worked with a ghostwriter? I'm not sure, but they are super smart and probably could have come up with a way to teach what they learned *about* working with a ghost. Would they have sold as many seats if they explained that they spent a small fortune gaming the system to ensure their spot on the *New York Times* bestseller list? Again, no one can be sure. That said, they could have provided people with a realistic view of how hard it is to actually achieve that goal and helped them realign their expectations. They are so magnetic, they could have been transparent and still sold plenty of seats.

Hype, false hope, and unrealistic promises lead to a sea of broken hearts and empty bank accounts. You don't need to add adjectives, superlatives, or zeros to be enough. It's okay if you don't have the perfect life. It's okay if you still face the same challenges you want to help readers handle. It's okay if you're a work in progress, if you're still working on realizing your own dreams.

You don't have to offer the moon to get people to read your book.

In this chapter, you'll learn how to craft a Promise you can deliver.

Your Promise Is a Sacred Contract

Your reader wants you to be right. They want you to have the answers, the way, the ideas, the plan. The reader who finds your book and chooses to buy it is doing so because they are hopeful. Hopeful that you have all the answers. Hopeful that you can show them the way. Hopeful that there is a path toward what they want. Hopeful that you know how to help them get unstuck. Something in your book summary convinced them that you have information they need that can help them. Readers give up on books for many reasons, but if you can build trust with them early on and show them that you do have the answers, or some answers—a path, a way that could help them get what they want—they will stay with you. They want you to be right.

Authors promise outcomes. You see it in their subtitles, in their marketing copy, and in their introductions. But are those outcomes doable? Can they actually deliver on their Promise?

Your Promise to your readers is more than marketing copy—it's a sacred contract. This is not about the $24.95 they pay to buy your book. It's not even about the time they invest in actually reading it. It's about the faith they put in you. It's about the hope. And that hope is precious. For some of your readers, reading your book is their *last* hope. They may be at the end of their rope, out of options and ideas. They may be desperate for a solution. They may have read ten crappy books on the topic and even though they are skeptical and don't believe a book can fix their problem, a tiny piece of them hopes that this book, your book, can be *the one*.

That's a lot of pressure. I get it. But if you honor your readers' tiny hope, if you hold their faith in you as sacred, your book will automatically be better. Why? Because you are not going to promise something you can't deliver and you are going to make damn sure that whatever you do promise, you *can* deliver.

Your Promise to the reader is the change, growth, or understanding your book provides if they buy it, read it, finish it, and act on your advice—by the time they turn the last page. Not ten years from now. Not eventually. *By the time they turn the last page.*

Many authors promise big stuff that can be achieved eventually. You can absolutely talk about the long-range benefits of reading and acting on the advice in your book, but the Promise is about right now, within these pages. What can you promise? A mindset shift? Relief? Comfort? A way forward? Peace of mind? A plan? Knowledge they need?

My Promise to you is, by the end of this book you will have a framework to help you craft a book that people read, love, and rave about. I can safely make this Promise. However, I *can't* promise that you will make six or seven figures from book sales, or even from other revenue related to your book. I can't promise that your book will win awards, or launch you onto the keynote stage, or make you a household name.

And I can't promise you that your book will be a legit bestseller (as opposed to an Amazon bestseller, which anyone can achieve by selling just a handful of books or pamphlets). Too many factors and variables are at play here—namely you. Maybe that will happen for you. Maybe it won't.

I do know the chances of earning big bucks, and of your book winning awards and becoming a *perennial* bestseller, are greatly improved when you write a book that delivers on its Promise. And I know that whatever book you were going to write when you sat down to read this book will be better for what you've learned here. It might even be great. It will surely be transformational for your reader, and that can only lead to positive outcomes for you.

When you offer a Promise that can solve a reader's problem and/or help them get something they want, and that Promise is realistic and doable, you honor that sacred contract and build trust with the reader.

Remember the Reader Transformation Sequence?

Buy. Readers will buy your book because you have a solution for their problem.

Read. Readers will read your book because you see them and you get them.

Finish. Readers will finish your book because they trust you.

Act on. Readers will follow the advice in your book because you believe in them.

Tell. Readers will tell people about your book because *they* believe in *you*.

When your reader trusts that you will deliver on your promise, they will finish your book. That's their part of the sacred contract—they can't get the promise if they don't read your entire book.

WORKSHOP: CRAFT YOUR PROMISE TO THE READER

AS I SHARED above, your Promise to the reader is the change, growth, or understanding your book provides if they buy it, read it, finish it, and act on your advice—by the time they turn the last page. So, what can you reasonably promise the reader will achieve if they a) read your entire book and b) follow your advice?

To start, go back to your Reader Statement and look for clues. Start with the answer to the second question: **As it relates to your topic and/or expertise, what does your reader want?** Now consider, can you deliver what they want in the pages of your book? Or could you get them at least part of the way?

You may also find the answer in the way the reader would describe their core problem. Is your Promise a solution to that problem? Relief from that problem? Tools to handle that problem?

You'll find other clues in the answers to the questions you answered in your Reader Profile from your reader's point of view:

"I would be happy if

_____."

"I would be successful if

_____."

Sometimes my authors discover their Promise is right there in the answers and only needs a little tweaking. More often, they need time to noodle it.

Now look at your answers to the burning questions and chief concerns. Do you see any patterns there that reveal what your readers want most? What can you fix? What can you address? How can that lead to one Promise?

Looking at your notes, start to craft one clear sentence that starts with, "By the end of this book you will . . ." You don't want a laundry list of awesome—you're not promising all the things. Understand the difference between a Promise and rewards. Michael Port, co-founder of Heroic Public Speaking and author of the must-reads for any speaker, *Steal the Show* and *The Referable Speaker*, explained to me that, in a speech, the Promise is what the audience gets if they adopt what he calls the big idea. Rewards are the specific gains the audience could experience *because* that Promise has been fulfilled.

So, for example, you might promise your reader that they will learn how to navigate conflict with ease. The rewards for achieving that Promise could be better relationships, the ability to solve problems quickly, stronger teams at work, increased confidence, and so on. Your reader likely wants a lot of rewards, too, but you don't have to list them for the reader to find your Promise compelling. The key is to zero in on the main thing your reader wants and then make sure you can deliver it.

Plan to spend thirty to sixty minutes on the first draft of your Promise. As was true for your Core Message, you will likely need more time to tweak it after you've jotted down your first attempt. Expect to tinker with it, to ponder different versions. This sacred contract with your reader cannot be rushed.

You'll know you're ready to move forward when your Promise meets these requirements:

Aligned. Does your Promise align with what your reader wants most?

Brief. Is it one clear sentence? Just as I asked you to come up with a clear Core Message that could be easily remembered, your Promise must be short and easy for you to recall and share. (Good thing you know not to include the laundry list of awesome.)

Deliverable. Can you deliver on this Promise by the end of the book?

The Promise is the last component of what will become your Content Filter, a tool I developed that works like magic to help you make decisions about which content goes in this book and which content belongs somewhere else—maybe in your next book. And your Promise is the key to creating a transformational outline. In the next two chapters, you'll learn how to do both.

When You Haven't Lived Your Promise

Sam Horton-Martin is a dear friend of mine who joined Top Three Book Workshop about six months after his beloved husband, Wayne, passed away from pancreatic cancer. From Wayne's first treatment and all through his last days, Sam had kept a journal on his phone, and he wanted to share his stories in a memoir so he could inspire other grieving spouses to create a new life without their loves.

In the early weeks of workshop, he developed his book as follows.

Ideal Reader: "Newly widowed people who want to create a new life without their spouse, who are struggling with the navigation of grief and may not realize they first need a shift in perspective about their 'unfinished' love story."

Core Message: "Happily ever after is right now."

Promise: "By the end of this book, you'll know you can create a life you love."

I had known Sam and Wayne for years, and if anyone had a story-book romance, it was them. Decades after missing out on a relationship, they found each other again by chance and married a few years later. I won't tell that story here; I'll let you read about it in his book. They were only four years in to their happily ever after when Wayne got his diagnosis. It seemed so beyond cruel, beyond heartbreaking.

So, when Sam landed on "happily ever after is right now" for his Core Message, goosebumps popped out on my arms and tears sprang to my eyes.

He spent the next few months writing and organizing his content. I waited for him to schedule an outline session with me, but he kept putting it off. He had loads of reasons.

First it was: "Some of my notes are in weird places. I have to gather everything."

And then it was: "I downloaded all my files from a software program and now I wish I'd never used it, because it's just one long string of text in Microsoft Word. I have to sort that out first."

And finally, he gave up: "I'm feeling overwhelmed with all my content. I need to take a break."

Soon Sam stopped talking about his book.

Then one day, when I asked him about it, he admitted, "I just don't see how I can write this when I'm not actually *living* a life I love."

Sam wanted to deliver on his Promise to the reader, but he hadn't yet delivered it to himself. Grief is wily, and some days it knocked him out. He had convinced himself that he could move on, and then waves of pain would wash over him. Some days, inertia won. Most days, he struggled. How could he be an example for readers?

I gave Sam space. Books come in the time they need to come.

Then, about fourteen months after Wayne passed, I sent him a text.

Me: "Do you think that maybe your book is not for recently widowed people, but for people who have a terminally ill spouse? Your Core Message would align better and you won't feel like you need to be at a certain point to write it."

Sam: "What you've said above sums up my heart's message so perfectly. I've been stuck writing-wise because I am struggling so much and my original Core Message hasn't been working. I'm a hot mess. Hot messier than I was even in the beginning. 'Life you love...' Not-so-much currently."

(Yes, Sam does text with proper grammar and punctuation. Also paragraph breaks.)

He had wanted to create a life he loved, and so he decided to forge ahead and make that Promise to the reader. Then he got stuck, because he wasn't there yet himself.

Sam thought about his Promise for a couple more months. And then he called me.

"I don't think my first book is for people with terminally ill spouses," he announced. "I think my original reader is still my reader. I'm not living a life I love yet, but I do know how to get through and start to live again. And the way I do that is, well, I haven't moved on. I just have a different relationship with Wayne now. I ask him for guidance. I talk to him. And that's how I get through it. I want readers to know that their relationship with their love isn't over just because they died. It's just changing."

"You know what that is, right? That's your new Core Message."

"Yes. That feels right," Sam said with conviction.

"So, what can you promise the reader?"

"That you can begin to live again."

Sam went on a windy road to try to come up with a Promise he could actually deliver to the reader, and in doing so, he revisited his Reader Statement and Core Message, too. This is not a common path for my authors, but it does happen.

Sometimes authors express concern that they haven't accomplished enough yet to make a Promise, or even to write their book. They think they need to be a fully fleshed out "after" picture to earn their right to be an author. Not so. Every one of us is a work in progress. Even if you're only a few steps ahead of your reader, that's okay. Just be honest with them about it. Let them know that you don't have all the answers, but you do know *this much*. Let them know that healing takes time, or that you still make mistakes and that you have more to learn. The reader will love you for it, because you're honest and transparent. And in your vulnerability, you show them that it's possible to get better—even if it's only a little bit better.

Remember, no matter how far you still have to go, your Ideal Reader wants to be where you are right now. Show them the way.

Your Book in the Wild

In workshop, I like to play the "pre-order" game. When I ask my authors to repeat their Reader Statement, Core Message, and Promise, I then ask the group, "Who needs this book or knows someone who needs it?" Usually, a lot of people raise their hands. When they do, I say, "Look at those pre-orders!"

I'll be blunt: I'm totally messing with your inner critic. I want to make that troll's life a living hell. For this exercise, I want you to post the following message on your primary social network:

"Do you know anyone who needs this book?"

Then follow it with your trifecta of hard-earned awesomeness: Reader Statement, Core Message, and Promise.

You're not looking for feedback; you're looking for people who *need your book*.

Please do this exercise. It's becoming real, you see, this book of yours. It's out there, in the wild, already lighting people up. A little pre-order confirmation can go a long way in helping you see that your ideas—and your doable Promise—are enough. It's good for the soul.

Onward!

CLAIM YOUR REWARD

Once you've completed your Promise, go to the Must-Read website (writeamustread.com/rewards) to unlock deleted content from this chapter and other cool and useful stuff.

Filter Your Content
with Three Questions

"**S**END ME EVERYTHING you've got."

Early in my ghostwriting days, I did most things the hard way because I didn't know any better. When I started with a new client, I always asked them to send me all the written material they had that could possibly relate to their topic. In addition to any writing they had already done, I received links to blog posts, transcripts from speeches and trainings, PowerPoint presentations, and sometimes photocopies of handwritten notes. Sorting through all that content was a bit like trying to put together a puzzle without the picture as a guide. Do all these blue and black pieces make up a whale in the ocean? A blimp in the sky? A rocket in the galaxy? Who the heck knows? Sometimes I felt as though I was drowning in words. I picked through all of it and tried to find a natural order to things. It took days, sometimes weeks.

Even after I wrangled their content into a cohesive flow, my clients had a hard time letting go of some of it. They acted like Steve Martin's character Navin in *The Jerk*, who, after losing his fortune, gets into a fight with his wife and tells her he doesn't need her or any of their stuff. Then he starts randomly picking up objects as he walks out the door, proclaiming: "I don't need this or this. Just this ashtray. And this paddle game. The ashtray and this paddle game and that's all I need. And the remote control. The ashtray, the paddle game, and the remote control, and that's all I need." Eventually, he's walking down the streets of Beverly Hills in a bathrobe carrying a bunch of random stuff, including a lamp and a chair.

My clients didn't need all their "stuff," but they didn't know how to part with it, especially if they loved it or someone else told them it was brilliant.

Eventually, I figured out that I needed a filter, some sort of tool to sift through their teaching, research, anecdotes, stories, case studies, and quotes and determine what belonged in my client's book and what could be used for something else. I needed more clarity. I knew what their books were about, but what was their specific take on that subject? I realized they hadn't really thought it through—and they were relying on me to do it for them. This is when I came to understand the importance of book development.

I started asking more questions about their audience, beyond demographics.

I asked them a bunch of questions to get at their main takeaway for the book.

I asked them about the key change they wanted for their readers.

Then I created a set of "rules" for each book, brief clarifying sentences that I could use for my filter. You know those rules as Reader Statement, Core Message, and Promise. And if you've completed the exercises, you are in a better position than I once was!

Next, I put each bit of potential content through my new filter. I asked myself three questions:

1   Does this content help me connect to my Ideal Reader?
2   Does this content support my Core Message?
3   Does this content help me deliver on my Promise?

If I could answer yes to at least one of the three questions, then the content could go in the book. If couldn't get one yes, I'd toss it aside. This process worked like a dream. Now I had an easy way to answer my questions, and my client's questions, about whether or not something belonged in their book. When you write a book about something, it can be so difficult to figure out how much you need to include. When you write a book *for* someone, it all comes down to what *they* need—what they need to feel connected to you, what they need to understand your Core Message, and what they need to get to the Promise.

The Content Filter also works if you don't have any content yet, or not much. You can use the same three questions to help you figure out what you need to create or gather.

Ask yourself:

1 What content do I need to help me connect with my Ideal Reader?
2 What content do I need to support my Core Message?
3 What content do I need to help me deliver on my Promise?

In this chapter, I'll break down each component of the Content Filter so you can easily apply it to your own stuff—whether that stuff is real or just kicking around in your mind. I'll also share some of my best techniques to help you find stories—from your own well and from those of others.

As you work through this process, you may feel the urge to plug your content into an outline as you go, or to skip this step and start with an outline. I ask you to trust me about the sequencing of this process and hang on. You'll start outlining soon enough.

But first, let me answer two of the most common questions I get from authors about content:

What exactly is a teaching point?

What's the difference between an anecdote, a story, and a case study?

What Exactly Is a Teaching Point?

When my authors start to organize and gather content, they usually have a mix of directive statements and "things they want to talk about." I want you to start converting your topics to directive statements, otherwise known as teaching points. It's just like it sounds—what you have to teach your reader.

Here's an example.

Let's say you jot down "Time of day to start a new habit."

That's your shorthand for a category of content you want to share with the reader, but what about that topic does your reader need to know? What is your take on it?

Teaching point: "For the best outcome, incorporate new habits into your morning routine."

Do you see the difference?

Going forward, I want you to use teaching points instead of topics, because your primary goal is to deliver on your promised transformation. Ask yourself what your reader has to understand so you can do that. By converting your categories to teaching points, you can easily see where you have overlaps and gaps. You can get the specificity required to figure out if you need sub-teaching points on that topic. And when you sit down to write that teaching point, you will have a much easier time fleshing it out.

What's the Difference Between an Anecdote, a Story, and a Case Study?

You've probably used the word "story" to describe not just stories, but also anecdotes and case studies. It's okay. Most people aren't sure of the difference. But I do want you to understand the distinction.

A *story* has three parts—you know them well. Beginning. Middle. End. In more accurate terms, a story has an arc. It goes like this: Setup. Conflict. Resolution. This is a simplified version of Plato's three-act structure. In act one, we get just enough information to know who the players are and the problem they are dealing with. In screenwriting, that problem is called the "inciting incident"—the event or situation that kicks off the adventure.

In act two, we have conflict and action. Stuff goes down. Stuff is blown up. Stuff is ruined. More stuff happens. It's the journey, the process, the trials and tribulations our hero experiences on their quest.

In act three, everything is resolved. The hero wins the battle. The girl gets the girl. The town is saved from the monster.

A story also has stakes. In other words, if the main character doesn't get what they want, if they don't solve the problem, shit will hit the fan. Bad stuff will happen. We're talking consequences, people. Real consequences. What is at stake for the hero?

When you look at the stories you want to tell, you'll discover that most of them do not fit these criteria. You don't have a story arc and you don't have stakes. What you probably have is a little tidbit about your life or a client's life.

Most authors think they have "a lot of stories," but what they really have are anecdotes. An anecdote is not a narrative and does not need any data. It's simply a short, incidental bit that is usually biographical.

An *anecdote* could be about your life or about someone else's experience—that of a client, colleague, family member, or friend. Sometimes amusing and always interesting, anecdotes help readers understand key concepts.

Let's say you want your reader to see the value of practicing kindness within their community. To do that, you've come up with a teaching point that is a different take on the saying "Good fences make good neighbors," a line from the Robert Frost poem "Mending Wall" and based on a proverb.

Your teaching point is: "Good neighbors who fix fences plant seeds of service."

To support that teaching point, you have this bit about a neighbor who, without being asked, fixed a broken fence for a single mom who couldn't afford to fix it on her own. You heard about this act of kindness from her son, who never forgot about that neighbor and now mows lawns and shovels sidewalks for elderly and disabled people in his community, free of charge. That's a memorable and poignant anecdote that does the job of proving your point.

If, however, you want a story to support the teaching point, you would need more information. Next, you call up the son. I'll call him Bob, for my uncle who passed away the year I finished writing this book, and once gave a homeless man the shoes off his feet in the dead of a Chicago winter because they were the same hard-to-fit size.

You ask Bob for more details about the story. Turns out, his beloved childhood dog, Henry, kept getting out of the broken fence. One time, someone found him and dropped him off at an animal shelter. Bob's mom had to scrape together coffee can money to "bail him out." They knew they wouldn't be able to afford to do that the next time he got out. Bob would lose his best friend. Now we have stakes. And, by starting with the time they had to rescue Henry from the shelter, we now have a beginning, middle, and end. *Now* we have a story. And to really bring this home for the reader, you include the epilogue, which is all-grown-up Bob doing service for *his* neighbors—without being asked.

A *case study* can have a narrative component, but the focus is on analysis. The problem, the approach and methods used to address the problem, any data related to what worked and what didn't work, and the outcomes—again, backed up by data. For case studies, include as much as you can about results. If you have testimonials, you'll want to ask that person for more information so you can fill in any missing data.

If you want to take Bob's story and turn it into a case study, you'll need to include research about people who are a service to their community. You might pull studies about what makes a person more likely to give to charity or to volunteer. You might have your own data based on a survey. At a minimum, you want to find out from Bob how many people he's helped over the years so you can show the impact (results) of his service.

I'm often asked how many stories, case studies, and anecdotes are required for each teaching point. I wish I could give you a magic formula, but it just doesn't work that way—not when you are focused primarily on the reader's experience. A good rule of thumb is to include at least one anecdote or story if you have a teaching point that needs an example, and more if that teaching point is complicated and may be hard to understand, or controversial, or goes against what the reader believes or has been taught. If you're sharing a process or system and want to show how it all works together, a fictional scenario could work just as well; simply give the reader a heads-up it's not a true story. You may need a case study if your reader requires data to prove that your teaching point works. Anecdotes are always helpful, and since they're short, don't worry too much about having too many. You can sort that out in editing.

Content That Helps You Connect to Your Reader

At a minimum, we don't want readers to feel alienated or left out. In a best-case scenario, we want them to say, "It's like the author wrote this book for me." When readers believe that you see them and you get them, they feel connected to you. When they feel connected to you, they are more likely to turn the page. To keep reading. And to follow your advice. Check. Check. Check.

When sorting through your "stuff" to determine if any of it would help you connect to your reader, look for the following:

- Personal stories that show you understand where the reader is *right now.*

- Personal anecdotes and stories that help them see you as a real person with flaws and fears.

- Anecdotes, stories, case studies, research, and quotes that help them see they are not alone.

- Stories and case studies that bolster their confidence.

- Anecdotes and stories that show how you or other people moved past some of their chief concerns.

Notice that almost all my examples have to do with anecdotes, stories, and case studies. This is because while you can address a reader's situation directly, it's easier to build trust when they see that you have shared experiences, or that you've worked with people who have shared experiences. This will require vulnerability on your part. You don't have to write about anything that makes you too uncomfortable or anything that would hurt someone you love. You have more gold from your own life than you realize.

Content That Supports Your Core Message

A transformational Core Message is the superhero of Core Messages, and superheroes need backup. Stating your foundational truth is not enough. You've got to prove you're right. Or, if you're not interested in being right, you've got to show that you're on to something.

Here's the type of content you may need to help support your Core Message:

- Teaching points and research that help prove your thesis.

- Teaching points and research that show that the prevailing wisdom is wrong, or the system is broken, or the guidance is outdated.

- Stories and case studies that provide social proof, evidence that your message helped others make a change.

- Cautionary tales that show that the prevailing wisdom is wrong, or the system is broken, or the guidance is outdated.

If you find it challenging to come up with content to support your Core Message, reverse engineer it. Think about how you came to realize your Core Message and the various other realizations you had along the way. Many of those aha moments are teaching points, and where there's a teaching point, there's a story that aligns with it.

Content That Ensures You Deliver on Your Promise

Of the three questions in the Content Filter, this final one is the most important. To write a book that changes lives, you'll have to deliver on your Promise. Period.

It's helpful to orient yourself to your Ideal Reader's starting point when sorting through your stuff. Do you have the following?

- Teaching points that help the reader shift their mindset.

- Teaching points that provide them with essential knowledge.

- Teaching points that show them how to do what you are asking them to do.

- Anecdotes and case studies that illustrate your teaching points and provide social proof.

- Case studies and research that support your teaching points.

- Stories that help your reader feel better about their choices, more hopeful, and more confident.

- Exercises/action steps that help them make progress.

You'll likely drop a few bits that you'd planned to include in your manuscript. Some of your content will move your reader toward their destination, and some of it is superfluous. Even more likely, you'll find big gaps in your content and come up with a list of stuff you'll need to create or gather to make good on your Promise.

WORKSHOP: BUILD YOUR CONTENT INVENTORY

YOU NOW have a simple way to cut through the noise in your head, the ideas other people hand you, and come up with a list of content your reader needs.

Your stuff. Considering all you've learned about how to choose what to include in your book, apply the Content Filter to your existing stuff:

1. Does this content help me connect to my Ideal Reader?

2. Does this content support my Core Message?

3. Does this content help me deliver on my Promise?

Stuff you need. Then fill in the gaps. Make a list of the teaching points, stories, anecdotes, case studies, research, quotes, action steps, and exercises you also want to include:

1. What other content do I need to help me connect with my Ideal Reader?

_____

_____

2. What other content do I need to support my Core Message?

_____

_____

3. What other content do I need to help me deliver on my Promise?

_____

_____

If you get stuck, you already have a tool to help you get out. Go back to your Reader Profile and turn to the burning questions and chief concerns. Then answer the questions and address the concerns. These responses can become teaching points and how-tos. Even if you think you have enough content, you may want to give this a try to help you fill in any gaps.

Sort your stuff. Finally, note which content you still need to create on your own and which content you need to find or gather from other sources.

Although there are only three steps in this workshop exercise, it may take you a few hours to complete it. If you have content in a lot of different places, or if it's not labeled in a way that makes it easy to find, it could take days.

You'll know you're ready to move forward when you feel you have _most_ of the content you think you need. Do not expect to get to 100 percent, to gather all of it; you'll never get there. If you are almost there, or close to finished, you're ready to move on.

Again, there is no magic formula for how much content you need, or how much of a specific type of content you need. Your measure is your reader and what it will take to get them where they want to go. If, after you apply the Content Filter, you still have a lot of content, or if the reverse is true and you don't think you have enough—don't worry. In the next chapter, I'll show you how to take the work you've completed in this exercise and shape it into a transformational outline. In that process, you'll likely pare down—or add—further.

Interview to Find Compelling Stories

Stories are powerful tools every writer should use. They help you connect with readers, provide social proof for your ideas and concepts, engage and entertain audiences, assist you in conveying your ideas and concepts, and provide the visual and emotional connection that makes your content memorable. A good way to find stories is through interviews. You can get a lot of juicy stuff from a conversation with someone who has lived some aspect of what you plan to teach.

As a ghostwriter and editor, I've conducted more than one thousand interviews specifically designed to find great stories for books. My best tip is to interview someone about a specific teaching point, not your general topic. In the first couple of years after I retired from ghostwriting, when I was still taking private clients, I helped an author's interviews by sitting in on them and asking follow-up questions to get at the details he needed. The challenge was, he had set up interviews with people who might have insights about his topic—leadership—but had not considered which people might line up with each teaching point. So the interviews started to sound the same. Everyone pretty much agreed with his Core Message, but there wasn't anywhere to go after that.

When I make a list of interviewees for a book, I have an idea of which teaching point they can speak to, rather than the entire book. Now, this does not mean that we don't do some exploratory interviews and others that are strictly on Core Message, but most of them are related to specific teaching points. If I'm short on stories, I'll look at the teaching point and ask myself if I know anyone who can speak to that— either as proof that the teaching point works or as a cautionary tale.

When you interview someone on a specific teaching point, you get focused, more specific responses. For example, let's say my Core Message is something like, "Before we can practice self-care, we first have to know self-love." (Oh, deep, Anjanette.) I could probably get a couple of decent interviews on that Core Message, but if all my interviews focus on it, I'm going to get more of the same.

However, if I interview people on a teaching point, such as self-care is a team sport, meaning, you need your family and friends to support your self-care, I'm going to get a good story specific to that teaching point, that *supports* the Core Message. Now, I interview someone based on that specific point, and I get to hear fun stuff about how her family prioritizes her self-care—a space they created for her, or a block of time when they don't bother her, or a check-in chart for her self-care that is monitored by the kids. And maybe you'd get a story about some not-so-fun stuff about how another family sabotages self-care. Perhaps examples of interrupting meditation time with constant questions, or dropping laundry in her yoga room, or calling for rides in the middle of a scheduled massage or therapy appointment. See? Now we have stuff we can work with, and that stuff ties back to the Core Message but is more specific to the teaching point. A bonus of using this strategy is that you give the reader lots of ideas for solutions or strategies they can use in their own lives.

Here is the process I recommend authors follow when booking interviews:

1   When considering who you can interview, remember that audiences learn from stories with both positive and negative outcomes. Cautionary tales are just as powerful as inspiring stories.

2   When you've identified someone you'd like to interview, contact them and ask for twenty to thirty minutes of their time. Be up front about the fact that you may or may not use their story, and that if you do use it, it will be shared publicly. Be sure to tell them they will

have a chance to read the content that mentions them to sign off for accuracy. This will put their mind at ease about participating.

3 Record the call, and be up front about it.

4 Remind the person of your Reader Statement and Core Message. Get some general comments about that, and then move into the teaching point you want to discuss with them.

5 Ask the two questions I use to help find the story. Frame them around the teaching point.

- How do you know this [teaching point] to be true?
- When did you learn this?

6 As you listen to their answers, be sure to ask for more details.

Sometimes every answer to your questions will be wrapped up in tight little phrases, the "looking back at it now, I realize" box. The thing is, that's not helpful because what you need is the story—and the unique insights from that story. You need the juicy stuff. You want to know about the time someone packed away the unworn baby shoes, or listened to the same Elvis song on repeat for six hours, or climbed fifty-six flights of stairs because they were afraid to get in an elevator. You want the memorable, defining moments.

One of my tried-and-true questions, the question that usually gets unexpected and delicious responses from interviewees is, "What do you know now that you didn't know before?" You'll often hear something like "ohhh" after you ask them, because it really is a good, deep question they likely have not been asked before. To be clear, the "before" is before the change—before they fixed the thing, achieved the goal, adopted a new belief system, climbed the mountain. This question will get you wisdom from your interviewees that you can share with readers. Those insights serve as proof in a more effective way than the summary of the story can achieve. Specific insights shared are much more powerful than the generic outcomes.

Which brings me to results. I'm not sure why we forget to ask about specific results, but we do. We rely on endings that are the equivalent to "and they lived happily ever after," but that's not helpful to the reader. Make sure to ask the interviewee if they have *specific* results they can share. If they saved their business, in what way is it different? Are sales better? If so, by how much? Did they eliminate their debt? How long did it take? They started dating and found the one? How many dates did they go on before they found that person? They lost weight and got off diabetes medication? How much weight and how long did it take them to lose it?

Sometimes it's helpful to ask interviewees about a day in the life before and after. Describe a typical day at the office before you started advocating for yourself. And, now that you speak up, what are your days like? You could also focus on just a morning. Or the last thing they thought about at night. Or Sunday afternoons. Or Christmas. Or summer vacation. Settle on something specific that they can describe before the turning point and after they made a change, and then make the contrast for the reader. This is super helpful because it allows the reader to measure the change by example, and it also helps them connect to the people you interview. The specificity is everything. Also, once you get an interviewee describing a typical something—day, workout, conversation—they will start offering up better content for you. When they start accessing memories, more will follow.

Here's another type of question to ask in interviews. When did you know that you/everything had changed for the better? When did you know you were out of the storm? When did you know you had fixed the problem for good? Again, you'll likely get a vague answer, so you'll want to pull the scene/moment out of them by asking questions about where they were, what they'd been doing that day, who was with them, time of year, and so on. Anything to jog their memory and get the details you need to write a good story.

Remember, not all interviews will work out. Some people just don't have much to share with you, and some people, no matter how hard you try, don't know how to give you what you need for a story. That's okay. Keep trying.

How Can I Protect My Book?

I can always smoke out an amateur writer, because one of their first questions to me is, "How can I prevent people from stealing my content?"

First of all, you can't. Unless you never share it. People steal, and they might try and pass your stuff off as their own. It happens, and you do have recourse. If you have a system, you can trademark it. If you have written content, you can copyright it. And then, you can sue whoever steals your content. But let's be real here. It takes a monumental effort to develop an idea and write a book—even a mediocre book takes a lot of time. To publish and launch that book is also a huge endeavor, so an idea thief would have to *really* want your stuff if they want to profit from pawning it off as their own. Professional writers, career authors, they know this. They also have a plan to finish their work and get it out into the world, so time is on their side.

Of course, people steal concepts and processes all the time, often unknowingly. An eager aspiring author once tried to hire me to ghostwrite his book, and when I asked to see what he had so far, he sent me an Excel spreadsheet full of quotes and concepts from leading motivational authors—some of whom I had already worked for, although he didn't know that. He wanted to build a book off what he had learned, rather than come up with original ideas or even his own *take* on their ideas. (I did not accept the job.) While you can reference another person's work, it should not be the cornerstone of your work.

So yes, take the usual precautions, but don't sweat it too much. Still, I'm not a lawyer—I can't give you legal advice and I can't stop anyone from stealing your ideas or plagiarizing your content. If you're really worried about it, please contact an intellectual property attorney.

Protect your stuff the best you can, and then focus on getting your work out into the world. And part of that is getting your *ideas* out into the world. Is this book of yours the first time people will hear your Core Message or learn about your process? Own your stuff and dominate your space with your message. Write an article, or several, that ensures people find you when they search the terms you coin. Create a video for YouTube. Get on podcasts and talk about it. Here's where you'll be glad you took the time to craft clear statements about your Ideal Reader, Core Message, and Promise—they make it easier for people to align your message with you and easier to quote you.

Does My Content Work?

When I was a ghostwriter, before I agreed to take on a client, I asked myself one very important question: Do they have "the goods"? I had learned the hard way that, when it comes to transformational books, many people wanted to promise big things, but few have ample evidence—or any evidence—that their ideas, frameworks, systems, tools, and what have you actually work. Let's be clear about what I mean by that. It's not enough that something works for you. To stand behind your Promise to the reader with confidence, you've got to make sure your ideas, frameworks, systems, tools, and so on work for your reader.

I'm particularly proud of *Fix This Next*, the seventh book I wrote with Mike Michalowicz. He came up with a tool to help small business owners figure out what to fix next in their business. For the book to work, the tool had to work. Now, to be clear, the tool worked for Mike, no problem. He wouldn't write a book about anything if he hadn't tested it in his own business and got results. That said, he's sort of a geek about business. He loves figuring stuff out. He loves metrics. He loves asking himself the hard questions. And he's not afraid to face the truth, even if it hurts a little—or a lot. However, most business owners are more resistant to change. The same is true of readers. So we knew that we had to have a simple tool that worked with minimal effort and minimal objection.

The first iteration of the FTN tool was a set of twenty-five yes or no questions, and the process was simple—or so we thought. On one of our writing retreats, we worked on refining the twenty-five questions for two solid days, testing them out on my business as we went through them.

A week or so after the retreat, Mike gathered a group of small business owners to test the tool.

"I got a lot of pushback," he told me afterwards. "The problem is, people don't want to admit that they have these problems, and so they are challenging the questions on face value."

So we went back to the drawing board. Over the next six months, we kept refining the tool. Mike pulled together focus group after focus group of small business owners. He did one-on-ones and shared the tool in big meetings of entrepreneurs. Each time, he would come back to me and report the challenge, and we would tweak it again.

Finally, we saw the results we wanted: his test groups no longer resisted the process, they embraced it. In fact, they were able to find the problem they needed to address next within fifteen minutes. We were able to get amazing results from entrepreneurs as we wrote the book, so we knew for sure that the tool worked.

Does your content work? Will it get your readers to "Promiseland"? Remember, our goal is to help the reader make a change. If our content doesn't help them do that, then what's the point? Take the time to figure out if your tool works with folks who are less informed than you are, less experienced than you are, less open to ideas.

One way you can do this is to take mini-breaks while you're writing your book to test drive your content. You don't have to create a big event or multiweek course to do this, and you don't have to test everything all at once. You could test a tool, like Mike did, or your entire framework, or a few key teaching points.

While writing her book *Delight in the Limelight* in Top Three Book Workshop, Linda Ugelow took several mini-breaks to test drive different parts of her content. First she took my course, Test Drive Your Content, so she could maximize each test and pull the best data. She then hosted one-hour webinars, weeklong open houses, and weekend retreats. Linda took careful notes and noticed when her content worked beautifully and when she needed to make improvements. This helped her refine her content for her book and her education offerings, which would be enough of a reason to test drive. But wait, there's more! Linda's experiments allowed her to keep her book front and center in her network because she shared the reason for the testing. And she easily gathered more anecdotes, stories, and case studies from participants that went right into the book. Test driving your content is a no-brainer.

Your Book in the Wild

In organizing the content for your book, you may have discovered that you need an additional story, anecdote, or piece of research. It's pretty rare that you have everything you need before you start writing, and it's okay if you don't. Look at this as an opportunity to continue to let your book live in the outside world and to make sure people know about it.

Today, I want you to pick one teaching point and ask someone—or a group of people, if you want to post on social media—if they know anyone you can interview about that specific point. You're looking for someone who is a good example of using that teaching point in some aspect of their life or work, or someone who did *not* use that teaching point and regrets not doing so (hello, cautionary tale).

By the way, this is a great way to start a relationship with influencers and other people who can help you out. Ask them, "Do you know anyone I could interview about this key teaching point in my book? Someone who uses this [philosophy, technique, process]?" Or "Do you know someone who has experiences with X?" That's an easy ask. Sometimes they'll say, "Me!" Sometimes they'll refer you to someone else. Either way, you've asked them for the kind of help most people are happy to give.

Onward!

CLAIM YOUR REWARD

Once you've completed your Content Inventory, go to the Must-Read website (writeamustread.com/rewards) to unlock deleted content from this chapter and other cool and useful stuff.

Create a
Transformational Outline

I N PRESCHOOL, we learn to sort like items with like items. Put all the trucks in one bin and all the balls in another bin. The crayons go in the crayon box and the markers go in the marker bucket. Move all the fruits to this side of the table and all the vegetables to that side. We often outline our books with the same mentality. This content goes with this content and that content goes with that. We think we'll just group similar content together and make those groups chapters. I call it the "silverware drawer method." Makes sense, right? Basic logic. Except that writing a book is not about organizing content. It's about creating an experience for the reader.

Grouping like content with like content is about as far as some first-time authors get before they hit up Google: how to outline a book. Try it and you'll get a lot of results offering templates and formulas. Templates make us feel better about outlining because writing a book is so nerve-racking. We worry that we're getting it wrong, and templates make us feel better. We look at tables of contents in other books and try to wrangle our content into the same framework. We study what everyone else is doing and try to make it work for us. Except the problem is, we may not be writing for the same or even a similar audience, and, more problematic, the author you copy may not actually have considered their reader at all.

Some templates are very helpful. Here's one I teach: Set up the problem. Explain why the reader may have had trouble solving it in the past. Give another reason why the reader may have had trouble. Present your solution. Prove it works. Show the reader how to implement it. Most make good sense, they really do. And if one of them works for you, by all means use it. The tendency, the very human tendency, is to choose one of the options presented to us. Oh, there are four types of outlines? Which one should I use? Which one would be best for my content?

The best outline for your book is the one that meets your reader where they are and takes them on a journey that leads to your Promise, delivered. That outline may be a template, or it may be something totally unique to you.

In this chapter, I'll show you how to take your Content Inventory and create a transformational outline that will help you deliver on your Promise. This is an imperfect process, and you will wonder if you're doing it right. As long as you keep your Ideal Reader firmly in mind, you are doing it right.

Your Reader Is on a Quest and You Are Their Guide

Imagine your reader is the protagonist in an adventure movie. They are on a quest to find their true love, to save the house, to win the choir competition, to slay a dragon. Instead of Obi-Wan or Rocky's coach Mickey, your book appears on their doorstep along with a letter that reads: "You have been chosen to complete a quest. This book has (nearly) everything you'll need on your journey."

In the movie, your reader uses the book to find their way (map included!), to learn mysterious truths, to gain wisdom and strategies and tools. They also encounter danger, roadblocks, and challenges. At each turn, they open your book for answers.

Okay, if that's too dramatic for you, how about this: You know the map kiosks at the mall that show you where you are in relation to Macy's or the hot dog stand? I want you to think about your reader's "you are here." Where is your reader right now on their journey? And how are you going to get them to Macy's through a mall full of crowds, noise, and distractions?

Your reader is on a quest. Even if that quest is for something simple or practical, it's still a quest. And you are their guide. You are not the hero of this book. They are. You are not the focus of this book. They are. And they need you to help them get where they want to go.

Sequencing: The Progression of Thought

On the Ideal Reader's journey, information unfolds. I call this the Progression of Thought. I started using this term to explain how to sequence a book when I was a ghostwriter and didn't know any fancy, official terms. The Progression of Thought is the natural way your Ideal Reader processes your teaching. Think of it like a conversation you have a with someone to try and show them how to do something, or to persuade them to consider your point of view.

This conversation happens over the course of the entire book *and* in each chapter. Each chapter should have a key takeaway, and you need to ensure your reader understands and believes it before you can move on to the next chapter. Within each chapter, you have that same unfolding of knowledge, that same Progression of Thought.

Sequencing is perhaps the most challenging aspect of writing a book. It takes a lot of practice to do it well, so if you struggle with this process, please give yourself a giant break. Most of my students have a hard time figuring out how to sequence, and I've come to believe it's because it's easier to see the full picture when we have a first draft to work with. As you write and as you edit, you will make adjustments, so do your best for now. Remember to leave the silverware drawer behind and focus on your Reader Journey.

The Job of the Introduction vs. Chapter 1

When outlining your book, you may wonder what to include in the introduction and what to include in Chapter 1, and how much overlap is okay. Add to the confusion the anecdotal theory that "most people don't read intros," and now you have a real conundrum. Should you include an intro at all? Should it be short? Should you just give up now and let a ghostwriter sort this out?

Here's the anatomy of an intro and Chapter 1, the must-have internal organs, as it were.

Introduction:

- An anecdote, short story, or relatable scenario that helps you connect with your reader where they are and shows you understand what they want and the main challenge/problem standing in their way. (Think Reader Statement.) It's helpful if this story shows you in an authoritative role, such as coach, speaker, consultant, and so on.

- Any statistics you may have that help the reader feel that they are less alone, because X percentage of people/businesses/couples/ what have you also experience this same challenge.

- Your mission/passion for helping the reader and people like them (why you wrote this book) and a bit about your experience working with these people (credentials shared in an organic way).

- The solution to their problem, which leads to the introduction of the Core Message.

- And you know the Core Message is true because you have X, Y, Z social proof. (This is a summary, not stories.)

- The Promise of the book.

- Any required management of expectations regarding that Promise.

Chapter 1:

- A story or relatable scenario that either mirrors the reader's pain points right now or shows them the Promise fulfilled.

- The reader's problem as they would describe it.

- Because of this problem, the reader has tried X, Y, Z solutions that didn't work.

- Those solutions didn't work or work as well as they could have because A is really (or also) standing in their way.

- The key understanding they need is the Core Message.

- You know this is true because . . . (Core Message origin story).

- And you can prove it with these social proof stories or anecdotes.

- If your book has a step-by-step process or a framework, include an overview of that process or framework.

- If they read your book, they will reach this Promise (hope).

You can skip the intro if you want to. It is not a requirement to write one. When in doubt, always come back to Reader First. Do they need one? If you do skip your intro, you may want to include some statistics and a bit more about you in the first chapter, though we aren't looking for a CV here. Your bio will cover most of it.

Think of your introduction as presenting you and your Core Message and the first chapter as making a case for it. Share your Core Message in the intro, but in Chapter 1, explain it and back it up as best you can so the reader will keep reading.

I've found that my authors need to be reminded to include the Core Message in their first drafts. Even after hearing it a bunch of times, they submit first chapters with no sign of it! I think it's because they doubt themselves. Don't bury your brilliance. Shine a spotlight on your Core Message. It's yours, it's a big deal, and it deserves prime real estate in Chapter 1.

WORKSHOP: BUILD YOUR WORKING TRANSFORMATIONAL OUTLINE

NOW THAT you understand you are your Ideal Reader's guide, you can think about the order in which they need your information on their journey. I have a systematic approach to finding a home for different types of content. You're going to build your transformational outline like decorating a Christmas tree. If you don't celebrate Christmas, I'll give you the basics:

1 First check to make sure the lights and ornaments aren't broken.

2 Next, add the lights to the tree. Start from the bottom and work your way up.

3 Now add the heavy ornaments at the bottom.

4 Then place the rest of the ornaments on the tree, with the lightest ornaments on toward the top.

5 Look for gaps and fill them in.

6 Add tinsel, if that's your thing.

7 Place the star or angel on top of the tree.

Outlining is pretty much the same, though we have a tendency to do it in the wrong order. We often start with our personal life story and then apply the "silverware drawer method" for the rest of our content because that's how our brains want to organize it. *Bzzz.* (That's the "wrong answer" button, in case you're wondering.)

So, what is the right order?

1 First check to make sure the content in your final inventory actually serves your reader. You can do this using the Content Filter (see Chapter 5).

2 Next, sequence teaching points.

• Outline your introduction and first chapter as described in the previous section.

• Then, pull your teaching points and put them in order of what your reader needs to know first, then next, then next, then next. This will take you some time, so be patient with yourself.

• You'll notice that some of your teaching points have sub-points that dig deeper. This is a clue that it could be a main takeaway for a chapter. Start to label the main teaching points as chapters. You may combine some of them, even with sub-teaching points, and that's okay. This is just a start.

3   Now layer in the stories that connect to teaching points, to provide clarity and social proof. Remember, you don't need a story for each teaching point and some teaching points may need more than one.

4   Then add the rest of the stories that are designed to help you connect with your reader and provide entertainment value.

5   Look for gaps and fill them in. What else does your reader need for you to deliver on the promise?

6   Add supportive research, if you need it.

7   Add action steps, if you need them.

What you want in the end is a numbered list of chapters. Each chapter should have a main takeaway and a bulleted list of related teaching points and stories, as well as any other content (anecdotes, case studies, research, action steps, and so on) that supports that takeaway.

Note: Your first attempt at outlining will likely include a long runway to get to the good stuff. Don't do that. Although we want your reader to finish the book, many won't. This is why it is important to front-load your book with the Core Message and an overview of your framework or process, if you have one. Don't make your reader work for it by slogging through several "setup" chapters before they get to the content that will help them make a change. For example, if you have two mindset chapters up front, consider weaving that content into later chapters.

Some of my workshop participants use a spreadsheet to build their outline; some use mind-mapping software; some use good ol' Microsoft Word. The way I like to outline is with Post-it notes. Give it a try—the results may surprise you. You can transfer your outline to any medium you like after you're done.

1   Get a pack of multicolored Post-it notes.

2   Choose one color for teaching points, one for stories, one for research, one for action steps/exercises, and so on. Remember, only account for the types of content *you* plan to use.

3   Then, on a wall or posterboard, start building your outline using the method I detailed above.

4   When you're done, sit back and look at your visual outline. What do you see? Do you have too much of one color? Too little? This is an easy way to identify gaps or notice where you may have too many stories in a row, for example.

5   Because you're using Post-its, you can shift content around easily. You can also look at your outline for inspiration. I find it very helpful to turn in my chair and eyeball my outline this way.

A few words about expectations. Keep in mind that this process can take some time. I can usually bang out an outline in an afternoon, but that's because I've done this more times than I can count. Plan to give yourself at least a weekend—preferably a couple of weeks—to tinker with this process off and on. You'll notice things you want to shift when you step away and come back to it. That's normal.

You'll know you're ready to move forward when your content is organized into chapters and you feel excited to start writing.

Your outline will change. You'll tweak it while you write. You'll tweak it while you edit your draft. And you'll tweak it when you work with your developmental/substantive editors (more about that in Chapter 9). All of that is normal and to be expected, and it's perfectly okay. The goal here is to get an outline that is about 80 percent there, enough so that you can start to write and you have a pretty good idea where you want to lay down those words.

As a reminder, I documented my process in creating this book for you on video, using screen share. You can see me complete each workshop section in my Behind the Book video series, which is free to download from my website (writeamustread.com/behindthebook). I've found that my authors understand the outlining process better when I show them how to do it, so I included that process in the video series.

Early Wins

Once you have your basic outline complete, look for places to provide your reader with "Early Wins." Remember, you want them to finish reading this book, so you've got to give them incentive. An Early Win is usually an easy-to-complete task that gives your reader a feeling of accomplishment and a result that shows your process works. A good example of an Early Win is the first time I asked you to share "your book in the wild." In Chapter 2, I encouraged you to announce that you are writing a book and to post your Reader Statement on social media.

Keep your Early Wins as simple as possible. They don't qualify if your reader must jump through a lot of hoops to complete them. For example, in *Profit First*, Mike asks readers to open one bank account and start transferring 1 percent of each deposit into that account. Now, there are several Profit First accounts, and we started out asking the reader to open all of them. Then we realized this was asking too much of the reader. So we simplified it. This simple action gave the reader such a profound sense of accomplishment, they kept going. And as their profit account accumulated funds, that feeling grew.

Where can you give your reader Early Wins?

The Reader Journey

Let's use the Hero's Journey approach to think differently about the reader experience, the Reader Journey. If you aren't familiar with it, Joseph Campbell, a professor of literature who studied myth and religion, coined the term for common adventure stories. He broke it down into seventeen stages. For a good example of a story that follows Campbell's stages to the letter, watch the original *Star Wars*, the one where Luke, Leia, and Han Solo meet. Christopher Vogler, a screenwriter, simplified it further, into twelve stages. Whether you go with seventeen stages or twelve, they fall into three acts: the departure, the initiation, and the return.

Let me be clear. I am not asking you to try and fit your outline into the Hero's Journey framework. I simply want you to consider it as you think about your reader's quest. Understanding how the Hero's Journey applies to *your* hero, your reader, will help you give them what they need to complete that journey.

To save time and brain power, let's use the twelve stages. I'm not a scholar like Campbell or a story genius like Vogler, so I'm not going to go deep on this. If that's your jam, by all means read their books and watch Campbell's interview with Bill Moyers, *The Power of Myth*. I do, however, know how a reader approaches a book designed to help them change. So here's my take on the Hero's Journey, as it relates to a reader's transformation in a book—your book.

1   **The Ordinary World.** This is your reader's life right now and their problem as they would describe it.

2   **The Call to Adventure.** The reader learns your Core Message and Promise.

3   **Refusal of the Call.** The reader thinks, "This won't work for me because . . ." and/or "I'm too scared to do this."

4   **Meeting the Mentor.** The reader decides to trust you because you have experience helping others do it.

5 **Crossing the First Threshold.** The reader decides to try and to keep reading. Note: All the above is generally in Chapter 1.

6 **Tests, Allies, Enemies.** The reader learns a new way of thinking and doing.

7 **Approach to the Innermost Cave.** The reader experiences setbacks: challenges, self-doubt, naysayers.

8 **The Ordeal.** The reader faces their biggest fears/greatest personal challenge.

9 **Reward (Seizing the Sword).** The reader experiences an epiphany.

10 **The Road Back.** The reader applies their new knowledge in the real world.

11 **Resurrection.** The reader faces their final test. Will they go back to their old ways?

12 **Return with the Elixir.** The reader's promised transformation is complete and they have a new perspective on possibilities. This is the end of your book. I call this the Call to Greatness, which you'll learn about later in this chapter.

It's useful to think about your reader experiencing the adventure that is your book, and how that adventure presents new challenges that ultimately help them make the change they want to make—for their body, their relationship, their mind, their business, their art, their sanctuary, their dreams—whatever Promise they seek in the pages of your book.

Your book is not a collection of stories and knowledge. It is a journey—a quest. Make this mindset shift and you are already on the road to writing something truly remarkable.

The Reader's Epiphany

Remember my story about dropping everything to "spend the day" with Steven Pressfield in Nashville? He talked a lot about the artist's journey and how it intersected with the Hero's Journey. He blew my mind when he shared his thoughts about two Hero's Journey stages, the Ordeal and Reward, and the epiphany. Seriously, I sat stunned and then took furious notes. What I learned was worth the cost of the event, getting to the event, and even apologizing to my wife about missing our Brandi Carlile date to go to the event.

Traditionally, the Reward is seen as the knowledge the hero gains from the Ordeal. This knowledge is attributed to a higher source, a divine source. Suddenly the clouds part and all is made clear, that sort of thing. Except Mr. Pressfield views it differently.

He said, "Epiphany is when you move from self-deception to grounded, not to a higher wisdom."

Whoa, what?

He went on to explain that it is after the Ordeal that the veil lifts on the hero's delusions, and suddenly they realize the truth—the truth about themselves. He shared an example from *Rocky* in which the night before his big fight against heavyweight champion Apollo Creed, Rocky Balboa goes to the arena and, in that moment, realizes he can't beat him. This is his epiphany. He's been kidding himself about beating Apollo. Rocky goes home to his girlfriend, Adrian, and it's then that he realizes that he may not be able to beat Apollo, but he can stay up in the ring. He can take punch after punch, because that's what he's been trained to do. He says he may not win, but he can "go the distance." Mr. Pressfield explained that this is Rocky taking the knowledge—the grounded wisdom—forward into the final battle.

Later, when I interviewed him for this book, Mr. Pressfield explained that he borrowed the idea of the epiphany from Jen Grisanti, who wrote *Story Line: Finding Gold in Your Life Story*. He gave an example from one of his historical fiction novels:

"I wrote a book called *Killing Rommel*," he told me. "It was a British Special Forces adventure story set in World War II. There's a scene in it where the concept of the epiphany just sort of fell out. I was writing a kind of internal monologue of the hero of the story, who is sitting around a campfire in the middle of the North African desert. The five or six guys around him have been fighting the Nazis, and these guys are real mankillers, you know? The hero is more of an academic type. He looks around and says to himself, 'I've always wanted to be like these guys, but I realize, sitting here, I'm not a killer like they are.'

"This is how breakthroughs happen," Mr. Pressfield explained. "You don't break through to some new thing. You rather give up a delusion. And, paradoxically, when the hero gave up the illusion that he was a mankiller like the other guys, it was the beginning of his true vocation as an officer."

Why does this matter to you? Because your reader will have at least one epiphany when the veil lifts and they realize the truth about themselves. You can't give this realization to them. Again, this is not higher wisdom (as in, from you). They must come to it on their own, and it's up to you to figure out where in your outline this realization might happen. Why? Because this is when your author needs you most. They need you most because this is also when they might give up on your book and on themselves—it's your job to stop that from happening.

Sometimes the breakthrough moment can lead a hero—your reader—to believe their own nasty inner critic-trolls. That they shouldn't bother with trying to change. That they can't do the thing. That they will never reach the goal, the dream, the better, more authentic life. And when this moment happens, your job is to acknowledge it in some way and bring them back from the brink.

All this fighting (boxers and Nazi-killers) reminds me of another construct of war/adventure stories I use to help authors deliver on the promised transformation. In my advanced Developmental Editing Retreats, I talk about the "Eve of Battle" speech that is common in war and sports movies. I share the famous speech from the movie *Miracle*, which I am partial to because most of the characters are from my home state of Minnesota. It's about the 1980 US men's Olympic hockey team that didn't stand a chance in hell of beating the undefeated Russian team, but still managed to pull it off, hence the title.

In the film, during halftime, coach Herb Brooks, played by Kurt Russell, gives an "Eve of Battle" speech to the team to pump them up and prepare them for the fight. At one point he says, "If we played 'em ten times, they might win nine. But not tonight. Not this game." I show my authors this speech and then I ask them to write their own version to help their reader through the epiphany.

Dr. Brooke Donatone is writing a book for people who want to learn how to deal with the difficult people in their lives. Their Core Message is, "When we make sense of things in the wrong ways, we make bad decisions and use the wrong boundaries." At the retreat, Brooke wrote an "Eve of Battle" speech for readers who, despite their growth after reading their book, may want to give up when anticipating the ultimate sparring contest for many American families: Thanksgiving dinner. My mother raised a pacifist, so I had been looking for a different way to describe this speech for a long time. Then the doc gave it to me on a platter. I now call it the "Eve of Thanksgiving" speech, and I hope you will, too.

Your "Eve of Thanksgiving" speech could pull your reader out of an epiphanic spiral and help them stay the course. Or a healing story could work, one that mirrors their own experience in that moment and shows them what is possible.

Finding and addressing your reader's epiphany is advanced-placement stuff, so for now, just see if you can spot a place where the reader may experience this moment. It could be when they realize they've been kidding themselves about their own abilities or experience, or when they must face facts about their past choices. Sometimes they experience frustration, shame, and fear, and sometimes hopelessness. Send them into Thanksgiving dinner ready to take on drunk uncles and conspiracy-theory-loving cousins. Lift them up off the ground and help them see their journey through to its beautiful end.

Call to Greatness

After I'd ghostwritten a few books, I realized that everyone ended their books on the same boring note: here is a summary of what you learned. Maybe they included some motivation in there. "You can do it!" Blech.

I thought and thought about it. A reader who doesn't give up on the book, who tried all the action steps and exercises, who made it through the entire journey deserves more than a summary and some pom-poms. This is no small feat! If the author delivered on the promised transformation, that meant the reader experienced a change. And if they experienced a change, that meant they had a shift in perspective that allowed them to see new possibilities. (Think the final stage in the Hero's Journey.)

When your reader opens your book, they have an idea of what they want. They have a dream, a goal, a vision. After they finish it, though, they are not the same person. So, yes, they are now well equipped to get that dream, achieve that goal, realize that vision. But what if there's more? What if their new perspective means they can dream a different dream, set a bigger goal, and create a more expansive vision?

Think of it like this. When your reader starts your book, they are at the base of the mountain. They can see what is right in front of them, and they can look at the trees, sky, and the mountaintop. When they read the last page of your book, they are at the mountaintop. Now, they can still see the trees and the sky, but they are *standing* on the mountaintop. From up there, they can also see for miles and miles, possibility after possibility. Without your book, they would still be at the base of the mountain.

So instead of a summary and a "go team" moment, I want you to think of the close of your book as a Call to Greatness. What can they do now that they've finished your book that they couldn't do before? Call on them to be more, do better, think bigger.

The cool thing is, your Call to Greatness can include a reminder of who they are now and what they are now capable of, which is an artful way to sneak in proof that you delivered on your Promise. You can also include a new story, if you like. But you *don't* want to include new teaching points.

To see an example of one way to write a Call to Greatness, skip to the end of this book.

Action Steps, Summaries, and Other Stuff You May Not Need

My authors know I hate journaling. Well, to be clear, I hate it when writers add a journaling action step in their books. Most of the time, it's fluff, a fill-in-the-blank shrug of an exercise. In my experience, the "journal for twenty minutes" exercise at the end of a chapter is there because the author couldn't think of anything else for the reader to do.

Of course, there are exceptions. Maybe it really would help the reader to write about their feelings in a notebook, or empty their brain every day. Natalie Goldberg got me in the habit of timed writing exercises with her must-read book *Writing Down the Bones*, and Julia Cameron, author of the classic *The Artist's Way*, got me and hundreds of thousands of people writing Morning Pages every day. Those habits helped me immensely. The thing is, Natalie and Julia *knew* that writing practice would be transformational for me, their Ideal Reader. They both had a reason for including that action step.

Look, there's no law that says you have to include exercises or action steps for readers. And there's no rule that says if you have an action step in Chapter 1 you must have one in every other chapter. When we try to write to a formula, we aren't thinking of the reader; we are thinking of the damn formula. We are trying to do what we think is right, what other authors do. I hereby give you permission to break the "rules." Please, please break the rules.

Here's how you know your reader needs an action step: if they do the thing, it will help them get what they want. That's it. Do you need them to try something, do something, or figure something out to deliver on your Promise? Then absolutely write that puppy. But if you don't, if you're just looking for something to include because you think you *should*, please leave it alone. Save it for a blog post or a video tip.

The same goes for chapter summaries. Does your reader need one to help them process your content? If your answer is no, scrap that item on your to-do list. Some of my authors use them and some don't. I'm not a huge fan of them, personally, but I do agree that certain types of readers need them. For example, my client Dr. Bob Baker wrote *The Performance of Medicine: Techniques from the Stage to Optimize the Patient Experience and Restore the Joy of Practicing Medicine.* He knew his readers needed a quick reference, so he included take-aways at the end of each chapter. He also repeated the takeaways in the appendix. Is this necessary for every type of reader and every type of content? Nope. The key here is to consider what *your reader* needs.

Reader First. Not shoulds. Not templates. Not other authors' ideas. Reader. First.

You may be wondering about other stuff you think you need in your book. Should you include a glossary of terms? A list of references or resources? Quotes from famous deep thinkers? Graphics, charts, or contextual models? You don't have to fret about these decisions. Simply ask yourself, "Would this serve my reader?" and you'll know what to do.

A Table of Contents Can Sell Your Book

Imagine this: Your Ideal Reader wanders through a bookstore. The title catches their attention. They pick up your book and flip it over to read the back cover summary. Huh. They are intrigued. Maybe your book has the solution they need. What's the next thing they do? They read the Table of Contents. What are they looking for? Confirmation that this book is for them. They need to see themselves somewhere in your ToC. They need to feel that your book may be *the one.* And yet, very often they find chapter titles that are meant to be clever, or cute, but don't tell them anything about what they'll learn. Or the headings are boring, so boring the book must also be boring, right?

Your reader wants to see themselves in your book. They want to see their problem articulated. They want to see their dream described. They want to see their burning questions (and/or the answers) and chief concerns (and/or the cures). Show them in the Table of Contents. Show them in your section headers, so when they flip through the book, one of those sub-heads jumps out at them and they think: "That's exactly the info I need," or "That's exactly how I feel," or "That's exactly what I want in my life."

Followed by: "I can't wait to read this so I can get to that part."

When you start outlining, it's okay—and encouraged—to use basic, utilitarian chapter and section titles. As you edit your book, put your reader first and amp up those titles so that when they find your book and check to make sure it's for them, they know for sure it is.

What If I Don't Want to Outline?

You may be the type of free spirit who really doesn't want to be pinned down by structure. You may want to figure it out as you go. I get that. I'm a longtime "pantser." If you've never written a novel, or done a lot of laundry while you tried to write a novel, then you may not know the term. A pantser is someone who writes their novel without an outline. In other words, by the seat of their pants. It's a process of discovery. Who is this character? I'm super curious. What will happen to these beautiful, flawed people? Who knows? How will this story end? Let's find out!

I used to say to my writer friends, "What's the point in writing the story if you already know the ending?"

Now, plotters, they're a disciplined folk. They map out their novels, sometimes down to the beat. Some write the ending first, which just blows my mind. I have nothing against this; it's just not my jam. I'll admit, I do plot ahead, meaning, I'll pants along and then plot the next few scenes or the next couple of chapters. This works for me—when I write fiction.

Nonfiction is an entirely different animal. I always outline (plot) before I write. Why? Because I have a different goal. With fiction, I am focused on honoring the characters and the story. With nonfiction, specifically personal and professional development books, the aim is transformation. My singular goal is to help the reader change their life, and so pantsing it is not an option. When I put on my ghostwriter or developmental editor hat, I move firmly into the plotter camp. Although that's a fiction term. What could we call ourselves, nonfiction writers who outline? Outliners is too obvious. Smarties? Ha. Maybe not. You let me know if you come up with something.

Your book's outline is critical for several reasons:

1 Writing is hard. Writing without an outline can be a nightmare.

2 To create an outline, you must consider everything we've talked about so far: your Ideal Reader, Core Message, and Promise. And, because you are committed to putting your reader first, you must also consider how to organize that content in a way that makes sense *to them*, that respects where they are on their journey right now.

The careful, thoughtful process required to create a transformational outline automatically makes your book better than it would be if you just started writing and figured it out as you went along.

3   Writing with an outline is more efficient. I often tell my authors, "Don't write all the way around the block when you could just cross the street." You will end up tossing so much more content—and writing so much more *new* content you didn't know you needed—if you start with your version of "once upon a time" and free-flow it.

4   Writing with an outline makes it easier to kick the inner critic in your head to the curb. This is not a minor point. When you pants it, it's much easier for the inner critic-troll to get in your head. *You don't know what you're doing. This is a giant mess and you'll never make sense of it. Who is going to read this gobbledygook?* With an outline, you know where you're going and what you need to do. When you've done the hard work required to get to the outline, you can just color in the lines. And when that wild-haired inner critic starts to bug you, you can simply turn back to your outline and remind yourself that yes, you do know what you're doing.

5   Building on the last point, when you have an outline, it makes cranking out the words much easier. In Chapter 8, you'll learn my years-tested, proven method for beating the mythical writer's block. For now, know that a carefully considered transformational outline allows you to write faster. I know, I know. I've drummed it into your head that you shouldn't hurry it up, that rushing to publish is the worst approach ever. I stand by that, *and* I know from experience that the book development process is crucial to writing a better first draft, fast.

Writing without an outline can be a hot mess of a process that will definitely impact the quality of your book, make a long process even longer, and may actually cause you to throw in the towel completely.

For the creatives in the house, do not fear. Outlining does not mean that you won't have room for discovery. In fact, I would argue that having a framework fosters discovery. An organized outline frees your brain up from having to think about where to put your content while you write. And it's easier for your brain to connect the dots when you've given it a framework.

When I look at an outline, I can see possibilities that I could not see when I simply had an unordered list of content. You can, too.

Your Book in the Wild

Just about the last thing most of my authors want to think about is marketing their book while they're writing it, but it's actually not that difficult. Truth is, you've already started. If you've followed through on the posting exercises from the last three chapters, congratulations: you've started marketing your book.

Readers love a behind-the-scenes look into your author life. My dear friend, the award-winning young adult novelist Julian Winters, says, "They eat that up." Pictures of your laptop or desk while writing. Photos of themes or people in your book. Your inspiration wall. Your messy bedhead when you wake up at the crack o' never to bang out some words. Readers. Love. This. Stuff.

So now that you have your Post-its, snap a pic and post it on your social networks. Don't worry about your intellectual property—most people can't read your writing, and if they can, they don't know your shorthand. For some reason, this picture of your content in multicolored Post-its or index cards is like a magnet for people. It looks so exciting (because it is) and mysterious (because they don't have a clue how to do it).

Show them the fruits of your brainstorm.

Onward!

CLAIM YOUR REWARD

Once you've completed your working transformational outline, go to the Must-Read website (writeamustread.com/rewards) to unlock deleted content from this chapter and other cool and useful stuff.

PART TWO

Draft

Momentum is everything
in a first draft. Get it done.

STEVEN PRESSFIELD

Write a
Super-Rough Draft

I T'S TIME FOR you to accept it: your first draft will not be great. It may have some good sections, maybe even some brilliant paragraphs, but it will not be a great first draft.

Good books have been edited multiple times.

Great, must-read books have been edited multiple times with the reader in mind.

It's funny—I say this over and over again. Other editors and book coaches say it over and over again. The Shitty First Draft (SFD), as coined by Anne Lamott in her must-read, *Bird by Bird*, is now a well-known term among writers and aspiring writers. We exhale when we are reminded that we *can* write an SFD.

And yet.

And yet we still somehow think we'll be the exception to the rule. In the recesses of our minds, we set the expectation that our first draft will be awesome. That expectation sets us up for disappointment, and that disappointment becomes fodder for the nasty inner critics, our trolls. I've found that while the reality of the SFD is super helpful (thanks, Anne!), most of my authors don't have any idea how shitty the first draft is allowed to be. If they don't think they're the exception who will write a masterful manuscript on their first try, they fall on the other end of the spectrum—they think their draft is the worst ever, so it is too shitty to be worth anything.

I remember one of my authors, Francesca Vavala, expressed concern about her messy chapters. She writes beautiful, soulful essays about her experience growing up with her twin sister, Emily, with whom she had been conjoined at birth. She'd send me a chapter draft that had a few tight paragraphs, followed by some notes to herself, then some details she didn't need, and no ending. Was I bothered by this? Nope. She had good stuff in there and some stuff she didn't need; she was missing a bunch of stuff and probably had more stuff to fix. The point was, she had *stuff*. Words. Ideas. Parts of stories. We can work with that. What we can't work with is a blank page.

"I guess I just wanted a clean, complete first draft to send you," Francesca told me.

"You're figuring out your writing process," I said. "You flesh out parts of it and leave other parts for later. You think about things for a long time, and then you come back to it. And you see connections after you have a good part of it written, and then go back and reshape it. All that is fine. It's *your* process."

So let me put these two myths to rest right now. Your draft is not going to be good *and* it's not going to be so awful that you should just toss it into a pit of fire. How shitty is shitty? Super shitty. (And now I'm going to stop writing that word, because I've repeated it too many times and my mom is going to read this.)

Just because you enjoy writing doesn't mean you automatically know how to put a book together. Even if you aced Honors English, even if you write other things well, the first draft of your book is going to need a lot of work. A lot. Way more than you think "a lot" is right now. Writing a transformational book is a specialized skill that you are not expected to know. It's a craft, and you are learning.

That said, you could end up with a less-shitty SFD. If you followed the Reader First developmental process in the first few chapters of this book, you abso-freaking-lutely could. Just by doing this important, clarifying work before you write, you ensure your draft will definitely be less shitty. It's just not going to be great. It'll still be a hot mess.

I want you to accept this truth for a very important reason. An unrealistic expectation for your draft is the surest path to an "incomplete." Most authors don't finish their books. They may give a host of reasons why—lack of confidence, lack of time, the fabled "writer's block"—but I believe that the underlying reason is almost always the impossible dream for their first draft.

If you don't know much about how a book comes to life, how the editing process works, you might assume that you have to get things mostly right on the first try. You don't. You simply need to get your words down on paper. Once you've done that, you'll make them better. After you experience your first editing pass, you'll start to see how you can make those less-than-awesome sections and stories into meaningful chapters. And the more you work on your manuscript and see the fruits of those labors, the easier it will be for you to lay down some really shitty words. (Sorry, Mom.) In the coming chapters, I'll show you how to do a lot of that rewriting and editing work on your own. And when you're reasonably satisfied that you've done all you can solo, you'll pass it off to your editor. You have many drafts ahead of you, so let this first one be less-than-perfect, okay?

I don't want you to join the "book-in-a-drawer" club. They have enough members. Millions. Maybe even tens of millions. So get comfortable with the fact that you are not going to love your first draft. Just keep writing. That's how you're going to get through this.

The First Draft Is Just Math

After moving to Los Angeles on a whim at nineteen, I accepted a job as a receptionist—my first of several "straight" office jobs I took to support myself. I had sold my car so I could have money to move to LA, which, in retrospect, was not a practical choice. With no subway yet, I had to walk or bus it to get anywhere.

At the time, I had been tinkering with an idea for a new play. I knew it had promise because the characters kept hanging around in my mind. And yet, a few months after arriving in LA, I still hadn't written a single scene. With a commute from Koreatown to Beverly Hills of about an hour each way, by the time I got home after a long day of work, I was exhausted and my feet hurt like hell. I'd limp my way past my first boyfriend, the handsome security guard who eventually dumped me for a green card marriage. Then I'd sidestep the stoner twins who hung out in the lobby, each with a yellow anaconda wrapped around their neck, and take the rickety elevator up to my studio apartment. By the time I walked through the door, I would have just enough energy to slip off my heels, open a pint of Ben & Jerry's, and curl up on my futon to watch *Roseanne*.

I remembered one of my mentors had written a play on his bus commute in Minneapolis, so I tried that approach. It was an epic failure. Most days, people squished in so close to me I could barely move my arms, let alone write legible words. By the time my bus pulled up to my stop on Wilshire Boulevard, I had a page full of manic-looking scribble that, if any of the psychologists at the mental health center where I worked saw it, they'd probably sit me down for a "check-in chat."

So I devised a plan. I would change my route home and stop at Rita Flora, a café/flower shop I loved at La Brea and 6th Street. I'd write at one of their high-top tables, surrounded by buckets and buckets of flowers, and I wouldn't let myself leave until I had completed my work for that day. The only wrinkle: setting time goals hadn't worked so well for me in the past. Every time I told myself I'd write for an hour, for a few hours, or for an entire day, I'd sit and daydream for a long time. A *really* long time. This was before the internet, and I still managed to waste time thinking when I should have been writing.

Then I remembered a story my dad had told me about how he passed his CPA exam. The test to get certified as a public accountant is no joke. The year my dad took the exam, out of more than one hundred candidates, he was one of thirteen who actually passed.

"I had three months to study for the exam," he had told me. "I knew how many points the test would cover, so I mapped out how many of them I needed to study every week. I also didn't want to study on weekends, so I then figured out how many points I needed to study each day."

In other words, he used math . . . to pass an exam about math.

I'm sure when he told me this story I rolled my eyes and did my best to ignore his advice. Now, though, I realized he may have been on to something.

I knew how many pages I would need to complete the first draft of a full-length play, and I had a goal to finish within six weeks. This was 1992, so no laptops around, not that I would have been able to afford one, anyway. My go-to was a ballpoint pen and a yellow legal pad. I decided I would write every day after work, and then, on the weekend, I would transcribe the handwritten pages onto my computer. This gave me five writing days each week, which meant I had thirty writing days.

Since I planned to write a full-length play, I would need about 120 typewritten pages. One page on my yellow legal pad equated to about half a typewritten page, so that meant I had to write roughly 240 pages by hand. From experience, I also knew I would cut a lot, so I figured I'd probably need another 60 handwritten pages to account for the scenes that would end up in the trash.

Here's how the math worked out:

300 handwritten pages / 30 writing days = 10 pages per writing day

Now I had my marching orders.

The first time I took the bus to Rita Flora and knocked out 10 pages, I felt as though I'd discovered fire. Knowing I had a page count goal somehow made it easier to stay focused. When my mind wandered, I'd remind myself I only had a few pages left to write. Before long, I slid off my stool, cleared my dishes, and headed back to the bus stop.

I pretty much floated the whole bus ride back to Koreatown. Yes, my feet still hurt. But when I passed my ex-boyfriend standing guard outside my apartment as I clutched my yellow notepad to my chest, I smiled a giant my-life-is-awesome smile. Almost nothing feels as good as a productive writing day. I even petted one of the twins' giant snakes.

That play would eventually help me make the finals for a Jerome Fellowship, which is no small feat, especially for a twenty-year-old.

More importantly, I had my first taste of how a bit of math and the discipline to back it up could help me finish something that would *eventually* become wonderful.

The first draft is just about getting words on a page that you will refine later; you need the most efficient way to do that. For me, it's remembering that the first draft is about the numbers—it's just math. Break it down and then tackle your daily goal. You can obsess about whether or not your book is any good later.

WORKSHOP: FILL OUT YOUR FIRST DRAFT CALENDAR

IN PUBLISHING, we don't count pages first; we count words. Get in the habit of considering your word count, not your page count. When you write to a word count goal, it makes it easier to write to a deadline. It also makes it easier to make steady progress, deadline or not.

You can calculate your word count goal in one of two ways.

Writing to a Deadline

If you have a deadline, here is the process:

1   Estimate your overall word count goal. Most transformational books fall somewhere in the 45,000- to 75,000-word range. You don't need an exact number. Just a guesstimate. For this exercise, let's assume you're going for 50,000 words.

2   Add 10,000 words because you will likely cut a lot of content. Now you're up to 60,000 words.

3   Set a deadline for completing your first draft.

4   Looking at your calendar, cross off the days you won't be able to write at all. Be realistic. Then go back and be even *more* honest with yourself about your schedule. If you have a big project due or a family trip, will you really have time to write? Maybe, but it's better

if you make it easy on yourself. When you don't write on a day you planned to write, it feeds your inner critic-trolls.

5   Add up the total of remaining days between today and your deadline. Let's say that number is 125 days.

6   Divide your total word count by your total number of writing days. This will give you your writing days' word count goal.

Here's how it looks in an equation:

50,000 words + 10,000 words = 60,000 words / 125 days = 480 words per writing day to complete the first draft by deadline

Writing with No Deadline in Mind

1   Here again, we start with an estimate of your overall word count goal. Let's go with that 50,000 number again.

2   Add 10,000 words for cuts. Now you have 60,000 words.

3   Determine your minimum word count for writing days. How do you come up with it? Over time, you'll figure out your average word count per hour. For now, let's go with my daily number: 300. This is my daily word count goal because I know I can hit it every writing day—even on bad days.

4   Now look at your calendar and note how many days per week you can write. When I'm on a project, I write five days a week. Some of my workshop authors write three days a week. It's up to you. For the sake of this exercise, let's go with my number: five days.

5   Multiply your minimum daily word count by the number of days you plan to write each week: 300 times five gives us 1,500 words.

6   Divide your total word count by your weekly word count: 60,000 divided by 1,500 equals 40, which is the number of weeks it would take me to finish a first draft.

7   Total up the number of weeks during this time period that you will be off for vacation or not be able to write much—or at all. For the sake of this exercise, let's say you need to account for two weeks of non-writing days. Add this number to the previous number. Now we have 42 weeks.

Here's how it looks in an equation:

60,000 words (50,000 + 10,000) / 1,500 words per week (300 words a day × 5 days a week) + 2 weeks = 42 weeks to complete the first draft

You'll need about thirty minutes to complete this exercise.

You'll know you're ready to move forward when you have a calendar that excites you, but doesn't make you want to throw up.

Now you have a realistic view of how long it will take you to knock out draft number one. You can tweak the numbers as you need to cut down on time—either raise your daily word count or write more days, or both.

I've made the math easy for you. Download your own Word Count Calculator from the Must-Read website (writeamustread.com/tools).

Paint-by-Number

Since I've managed your expectations on your messy first draft, I'm confident in telling you that it will be easier to write and it will make more sense *because* you did the essential book development work in Chapters 2 through 6. Now that you have a clear Ideal Reader, a strong Core Message, and a Promise you can deliver; now that you have organized your content and created a transformational outline that is "somewhat" ready to go, you can start painting the picture that is your book.

Have you ever tried a paint-by-number project? You know, the kits that include a line drawing of a landscape, a horse, or the Eiffel Tower, with numbered sections within that drawing. Those numbers correspond to paint colors in little plastic buckets. To complete the painting, all you have to do is fill in each little section with the corresponding paint color.

At this point, if you've done the work, that's pretty much how the first draft will go. You have your outline. Now start filling it in. Transfer your outline to a Microsoft Word doc. Yes, you need to use Word. You need to use Word because your editor will want you to use Word. And your editor wants you to use Word because it's the best way to track changes. No, don't try and argue with them. Just. Use. Word.

When you sit down to write, choose a teaching point, a story, or an action step you want to write that day and flesh it out as much as you can. You don't have to write in order. You can pick something that sounds fun. Or, if you're a "veggies first" kind of person, maybe you'll start with the hard stuff. Try to stay with each point or story and see it through until you have everything down that you think the reader will need to understand the content, and then move on to the next one.

Don't worry about transitions. Your sequencing is probably off anyway, and you can fix that and add transitions later. For now, just paint in the section that you know you need to write.

I laugh about this analogy because there are so many book "fill in" templates out there, and they are most definitely not reader-focused. The cool thing is, you have a template now, too, but *you* made this one. It's for your reader. It's not a formulaic outline you need to follow; it's *your* transformational outline. You designed it. So it's as though you first made the drawing, then chose the colors and labeled all the sections, and now you're painting in your own paint-by-number. Pretty awesome, right?

Write, Don't Edit

Your first draft is all about getting words on the page according to your outline. Remember, it's paint-by-number. Do not slow yourself down trying to edit as you go. When my workshop authors get stuck, I ask them if they've been editing. They almost always look down, sheepishly, as if I have revealed their secret. They know better, but they can't help themselves.

One of those authors is Susan Sandler. Author of *Midlife Magic*, Susan often waylaid herself by going back over her in-progress chapters.

Did she have work to do to make them better? Yes. But she had a hard time moving on. She wanted an almost-perfect chapter, and it just doesn't work like that. You might realize something you need to change in Chapter 2 while writing Chapter 5. And that realization could mean revamping a good chunk of the earlier chapter. If you have an almost-perfect Chapter 2, now you have to blow that up. It's a waste of energy.

"Tell yourself it's good enough," I told her. "Write that on a Post-it note and stick it on your computer."

She did. And she still does.

Editing gets you into judgment mode, and that can stress you out enough to make you want to give up. You may also start to get confused, and feeling overwhelmed can also stress you out enough to make you want to give up. You aren't showing your work to anyone yet, so don't worry about typos. Don't worry that you've gone on too long about a teaching point, or that you don't have enough details in your story. You can come back around and attend to that. If after a writing session you are nervous about something you wrote, leave yourself a note. In early drafts of this manuscript, you could find all sorts of notes I inserted to remind myself that I needed to fix something later.

Ideally, you want a complete chapter that explains and supports the main takeaway (teaching point) for that chapter and moves the reader closer to the Promise. That is your goal. Complete does not mean polished. It means you covered everything you planned to write in your outline. That's it.

Resist the temptation to go back over what you've written. Think of it as downloading information and stories from your brain. Just drop your content onto the page and *keep writing*.

Tell yourself it's good enough.

Leave Yourself Breadcrumbs

One way to slow yourself down while writing your first draft is to stop to look something up. Maybe you are searching for just the right word. Or maybe you forgot the year you went to camp. Or maybe you need to pull a statistic, or cite a source, or get the correct spelling of someone's name.

The best way to write efficiently and knock out as many words as possible on a writing day is to leave yourself breadcrumbs for that thing you want to find, change, fix, look up, or confirm, and then keep moving. Journalists have ridiculously short deadlines and they don't stop to look things up. They'll deal with that stuff after they have a first draft. They often insert TK in their copy where they will need to fill something in later. TK is an abbreviation for "to come," even though "come" doesn't start with a K. This is because you won't find many English words with that letter combo, so it's easy to find.

Some writers use "elephant" for the same reason. Unless you're writing a book about Africa or the circus, you should be good using that word as a placeholder. I use brackets because I almost never use them otherwise. I'll leave myself short notes in the brackets, long notes, whatever it takes. Very often it looks like this:

[Something about...]

Then, after I finish my first draft, I do a search in Microsoft Word to find the brackets and fill in whatever it is I left there. Sometimes I end up just deleting the brackets. The point is, I didn't get stuck worrying about finding the right phrase, or waste an hour or more down a research rabbit hole, when I should have been writing.

A bonus of this system is that it gives you something to do on days when you feel about as creative as a turnip.

My old friend Julie Anderson used to run a couture costume shop in Santa Fe on Old Santa Fe Trail. I'd bring her an iced coffee and sit and listen to her talk for hours, surrounded by the most gorgeous, elaborate handmade works of art you've ever seen. One day, she'd have some beading in her hand while we chatted. Another day, she'd be sweeping the desert out of her store. One time she said something I never forgot. "Some days, you can make a Queen Elizabeth, and some days all you can do is clean the toilet."

Some days, you can write, and some days, you can fill in the brackets. Either way, you're doing the work.

Storytelling Is Hard

I believe in the healing power of story. I believe stories are medicine, balm to our weary hearts. I believe stories are touchstones. I believe stories can cure the sick mindsets we all engage in from time to time, or all the time. I believe stories show us the way—to the dream, to the moon, to the cure, to the sanctuary, to the future. I believe stories show us the way home.

For the purpose of transformation, stories are essential. We hold on to them like a lifeline, proof that we are not alone, proof that we can do it, proof that what we want is not silly or improbable.

And yet, storytelling is a real challenge for most first-time authors and some established ones, too. Storytelling is a craft. No matter how many books you've read, it isn't likely to come naturally. So immediately, right now, give yourself a break. You're not going to be great at this. Not at first. You're probably going to suck at it. But with practice and intention, you will get better.

In this first, super-rough draft, get the story down on paper. And if you think you don't have enough stories, keep moving anyway. It's easier to see what you need after you've finished fleshing out the content you do have.

The Healing Draft

Mateo was ready. After learning about my workshop from a friend, he had requested a meeting with me so we could see if he'd be a good fit. He wanted to write a book that made a real difference, and he wanted to start yesterday.

He then explained that he had been abused as a child by a family friend and had spent decades living with the secret.

"I hope I can help other men who have been through what I've been through," he told me.

"That's very brave," I told him. "And how has your life changed since you started sharing your story?"

Mateo leaned back in his chair and sighed. "That's the thing. Most people don't know anything about it, and no one knows everything."

"Oh, wow. Have you written anything yet? And it's okay if it's random journaling, notes here and there."

"Nothing. I haven't . . . like I said, I haven't told my story."

"Not even to yourself?"

Mateo paused, then said, "Not even to myself."

Although he was eager to start the workshop, I advised him to hold off until he had a chance to write his Healing Draft—the first version of the story, the version that is just for him.

When we want to write a book that includes stories about trauma or other painful experiences we've had, it's important to first allow time to write those stories for ourselves, knowing we don't have to share the story with anyone else if we prefer not to do that. This allows us to use the process of writing our story as a tool for healing, to explore our pain on the page, with no pressure to create something great or even something that makes sense.

You are much more likely to give up on a book that hurts to write. Allowing yourself the space and time to create a Healing Draft first also helps keep the inner critic-trolls at bay.

I came up with the idea of the Healing Draft when Melissa, one of my clients who had signed up to be part of a collection of stories, asked me to write about her divorce. The problem was, she and her soon-to-be ex-husband were still negotiating terms and her feelings were quite raw.

When Melissa edited the first draft I sent to her, she added more than one thousand bitter words detailing her husband's betrayal. We went back and forth on the edits—I kept cutting her accusations and she kept putting them back in.

Finally, I said, "Melissa, you need perspective to tell a good story that serves readers. You're too close to it."

She was quiet for a few moments and then, in a voice almost too soft to hear, said, "I'm just so angry."

"I know. And you have every right to be. But two years from now, will you be happy with this story? Will you want your kids to read it?"

Melissa came around. She let go of the content that would not help her reader and saved her unresolved grief for a different page. And life got better for her. She moved on, and she's grateful she didn't submit a story that would have been a painful reminder of her past.

Sometimes you realize you've been writing a Healing Draft all along. Remember Sam, the author who struggled with his Core Message and Promise for his book for grieving spouses? He had started the workshop only six months after his husband, Wayne, passed away from cancer.

It was on the same phone call in which he shared his newfound clarity that he said, "I think I've been writing a Healing Draft all along."

He had wanted to have all his ducks in a row and get started on his memoir, but he kept hitting a brick wall. More than a year after starting the workshop, he looked back at his writing and realized he had been writing to heal himself, not to help his readers.

"That makes sense," I said. "You're past the first year of grief and now you're ready to look at your content in a different way. Remember, no words are wasted. The words you don't use helped you heal so you could write this book."

You may realize after you start writing that you are writing a Healing Draft, or that you probably should write one. Or maybe you'll realize that you need to hit the "pause" button and allow yourself to write a Healing Draft version of a specific story or set of stories. All of that is okay. It really is. Your process is your process. Take the time you need to write the book you and the world deserve.

Once you've finished your Healing Draft, then go back and figure out which aspects of your story would be most helpful to readers. Set aside what you need to keep for yourself and edit the rest.

Something from Nothing

I'm quite sure I couldn't have picked a worse time in my life to start a new business—and start writing in a medium I knew nothing about. At the time I made good on my promise to myself to never go back to my "straight" job, I had a six-month-old baby, five hours of childcare a week, and a raging case of postpartum depression. Oh, and we were broke. We lived in a fourth-floor walk-up in an "up-and-coming" part of Brooklyn that the gentrifiers called South Slope to align with the much fancier Park Slope several blocks over.

If you're not aware, a walk-up means no elevator. Imagine hauling a baby and all their gear up and down four flights of stairs, plus the twelve steps on the front stoop, so you can get to the coffee shop to write.

Now you're probably thinking, why didn't AJ just write at home? Well. Despite trying the whole cry-it-out, self-soothe thing, my son, Jack, only took naps in my arms. Unless he fell asleep in his stroller while we walked. I would stroll for about ten, sometimes twenty, blocks, and when he finally fell asleep, I'd double back to my favorite coffee shop, the one that let me bring the stroller inside, pull out my laptop from the diaper bag, and get to work. I could usually fit in about ninety minutes of writing time; two hours if I got lucky.

It was a terrible time to learn a new way to write and to start a new business. Most days, I walked for miles just to keep the scary thoughts out of my head. Jack wouldn't sleep through the night, and so I was exhausted pretty much all the time. Every day was a struggle to keep going, my only joy the sweet smile on his round face.

We had nothing.

I was sure I knew nothing.

I felt like I *was* nothing.

And then I made something. A book.

It was only twenty thousand words or so about a topic I didn't really care about. But it was a book. I scratched it out while Jack slept, word by word, page by page. One day it was a blank document with a blinking cursor, and then, several miles and naps later, it was done.

It was nothing, and then it was something.

And that something became more, and more and more. It became the basis of a new business, a new craft, a new life. A new me.

If you wait until the perfect time to write your super-rough draft, you may never get to it. You don't have to feel good to write. I've written through depression, anxiety, and sickness. You don't have to have an office, or a room, or even a desk to write. I write on planes, in cars, even on park benches. You don't need a lot of free time to write. For years, I only wrote when my son slept, and sometimes I only have twenty minutes to get a few words in.

Don't wait until you feel better, or have better conditions. Write anyway.

Let me tell you, the Brooklyn years were the darkest of my life, and still I made something from nothing. No matter what, if you just stay the course, you will, too.

Your Book in the Wild

Start posting your weekly progress on social media. How many words did you knock out? Did you figure out how to connect a story to a teaching point? How close are you to finishing your first draft? What are your wins?

Onward!

CLAIM YOUR REWARD

Once you've completed your First Draft Calendar, go to the Must-Read website (writeamustread.com/rewards) to unlock deleted content from this chapter and other cool and useful stuff.

Kill Your Inner
Critic-Trolls

MY AUTHORS started it.

About six weeks into my beta class for Top Three Book Workshop, one of my students held up a troll doll with pink hair. The next week, another student proudly showed off their troll doll, this time with purple and black hair taller than its body. By the end of the six weeks, almost everyone had one.

Their inspiration came from one slide I'd shared in class—a picture of a troll doll with bright orange hair, the same one that I had when I was a young writer. I showed them the picture to share a strategy I came up with to help me beat my inner critic. I needed some sort of creature that could represent the evil manipulator in my head that kept me from writing, so I could do bad things to it. At the start of a writing session, I'd sit the troll doll upright on my desk and then knock it over. Sometimes I'd say mean things to the doll. Other times, it would end up in the garbage can. That helped me separate my creative self from my inner critic. The next day when I sat down to write, I'd stand it upright and do it all over again.

Apparently, those first authors in my workshop loved the troll idea enough to take it on, and pretty soon, "trolls" became synonymous with the negative thoughts and fears that came up for them. Now it's a thing. A big thing. Most of them get their own trolls and do very bad things to them. While working on her game-changing book on sales, Carole Mahoney broke with class tradition and got an entire collection of poop emojis instead. She tosses them on the floor before every writing session.

I tell you this not because I think you need to run out and get a troll doll, but rather, because we have to accept that we have to deal with the inner critic in this process. Even if you think you've successfully banished yours to the basement, writing a book is like a fire alarm waking it from its slumber. Soon enough, your troll will be sitting next to you on the couch, telling you it's perfectly fine for you to binge-watch eighteen seasons of your favorite crime drama—again—instead of writing your words that day.

In this chapter, I'll give you some strategies to help you handle your trolls and forever free yourself of the mythical "writer's block."

Writer's Block Is Not a Thing

What I've Lost Because of "Writer's Block"—A (Partial) List

- The chance to get feedback on my writing from one of my heroes.

- A meeting with the writing team of one of my favorite TV shows.

- A playwriting commission.

- An offer to produce one of my plays.

- Numerous opportunities to share my work with people who could give me my "big break."

- An offer for agent representation.

- Two offers to publish my manuscripts.

- Three years of prime writing time while I wallowed in self-pity.

I SHARE this list with you for two reasons. First, to show you that when it comes to facing the famed "writer's block," I've been there, done that, got the T-shirt and the beer Koozie. I'm not one of those outliers who has no problem banging out five thousand words a day like clockwork. Those people are unicorns. No, I've wrecked things and caused myself extreme distress all in the name of being blocked, or not being inspired, or feeling stuck. Whatever you want to call it, I bought into the construct that has caused writers to, at best, abandon projects, and at worst, suffer from mental anguish and even take their own lives. Second, I share that list with you to show you just how destructive believing in the construct of writer's block can be.

Remember my "first draft is just math" story? I was nineteen and banged out the first draft of a full-length play in six weeks. By the time I was twenty, though, I had convinced myself that it was a fluke, that it only worked because "the characters compelled me to write their story." That's the lie I told myself, and then I told myself a whole bunch of other lies that kept me from making steady progress.

For more than ten years, I struggled with creating a career that lived up to my promise, primarily because I struggled with "being blocked"—sometimes for years at a time. The feeling plagued me. I started to think of myself as a choke artist, because every time I would get close to finishing something, I'd get stuck. But I also put off starting projects. I'd get so many ideas, jot them down in my notebooks with a flourish, and then just let them wither and die. You've got to nurture these little seedlings so they will grow. Without your care and attention, they just fall flat until you are looking at a notebook full of notes that mean nothing to you.

I used to kick myself—repeatedly—for losing everything on that list, but I've let all regret go. I've let it go because I figured out that writer's block is not a thing.

In 2004 I read *The War of Art* by Steven Pressfield, the book I brought up in Chapter 1, the book that changed my life. In it he explains the concept of Resistance, which he calls a law of nature, like gravity. When I learned this for the first time, it blew my mind. Finally, I understood why the nagging urge to avoid writing never left me—it was a law of nature, not something I could banish once and for all. What a relief! You see, I had come to believe that I had a chronic case of "writer's block" caused by something I did or didn't do, and there was nothing I could do about it.

False. I wasn't the problem. My avoidance—those hours staring at a blank page, those weeks and months ignoring the call to write— wasn't my fault. It was a law of nature, and now I had to figure out how to manage it.

If you're coming back to a manuscript you set aside long ago, I hope you'll give yourself a break for the months or years you let it sit unattended. If you ever chose to binge-watch a TV series or bake ten loaves of banana bread instead of writing, and then felt like crap about it later, let it go. If you've tried to write your book in fits and starts and give yourself hell for not being more disciplined, please stop. You didn't do anything wrong. It's not you. Really, it isn't. It's this damn law of nature, and it's the same for all of us.

In an interview with Oprah Winfrey on *Super Soul Sunday*, Pressfield explained how he deals with Resistance, and how he recommends we deal with it: "Put your ass where your heart wants to be." In other words, even if you don't want to write, do it anyway. Ass in chair, people.

I learned a lot from *The War of Art*. It also reminded me of everything I already knew, but either didn't realize I knew or had forgotten about entirely. For example, in the book, Pressfield talks about the little rituals he does every time he sits down to write. They reminded me of that orange-haired troll doll on my desk. Somehow, even when I was a baby writer, I knew I had to knock that inner critic over so I could write that day, and I also knew I had to put it right side up again to face the next time I sat down to write. Somehow I had sensed the truth about that inner critic years before. Somehow I knew that it would be back every time, good as new, ready to take me down, just as Pressfield said it would.

The troll was a zombie. I could kill it one day and it would be back the next morning. Once I understood that, I stocked my arsenal with all sorts of weapons so I could take that troll down over and over again, even if it brought reinforcements.

After reading his book, instead of focusing on all the times I'd failed myself and my art, I remembered all the times I hadn't.

I remembered a period when my oldest and dearest friend Zoë Bird and I would meet up at coffee shops in Minneapolis to write using prompts from Natalie Goldberg's must-read books *Writing Down the Bones* and *Wild Mind*. We especially loved the Theatre Garage on Franklin Avenue, just down the street from my apartment. It had a low-key grunge vibe and tables wide enough for both of us to fit our coffees and notebooks. We'd pick one of Natalie's prompts and write for half an hour or so. Then pick another, and so on. That was a super-productive time.

I recalled that magical time in LA, when I wrote ten pages a day, met my goal, and ended up with a play I loved.

I ran back over the year I thought I'd lost my voice for good, and then tried the LA math game again to get it back. I hadn't written in three years, and because I had disconnected from my stories, I had grown depressed and sad. So very sad. This time, I didn't have a deadline. I didn't even have an idea. I simply made myself write five pages a day after work, before going home. It was the reverse of Julia Cameron's famed Morning Pages exercise, which she details in her classic must-read, *The Artist's Way*. I sat in the coffee shop at Borders in Santa Fe, New Mexico, and wrote by hand in a small journal covered in batik fabric that looked like the night sky. Every word was an effort, every page a chore. And yet I showed up, day after day, and wrote my five pages. I recorded dozens of useless meanderings and then, like a tiny, fairy-sized gift that lands on your fingertip, I wrote a line that made me want to keep writing.

In the excavation of my writing life up until that moment, I finally understood the key elements I needed to beat Resistance:

- **Regular writing practice.** I didn't have to commit to a daily practice, or a certain amount of time. I just had to commit to a regular writing schedule and stick to it.

- **A focus on quantity**—words or pages. When I wrote plays, setting page count goals for each writing session worked like a charm. When I started writing books, I shifted to word count goals. Hence, "the first draft is just math."

- **Writing in community.** I knew when I had regular writing dates with friends and colleagues, I was more likely to show up.

Writing practice + word count goals + writing in community = my surefire cure for Resistance. It works every time. And so far, it has worked for every author who tries it. The combination is so powerful, I've seen some of my workshop authors complete first drafts in just a few months. More importantly, I've seen them get brilliant ideas and draw genius connections—all because they had a regular writing practice, wrote to a word count goal, and wrote in community.

In Top Three Book Workshop, we write together in writing sprints, Monday through Friday. We sprint for twenty-five minutes, break for questions and support, and then sprint again. At the end of the hour, we share our word count for the two sprints. Then we record it on a spreadsheet to track our progress. Five weeks into class, we start Sprintapalooza, a four-week sprint-fest during which we host at least twenty different sprints per week in the hope of making as much progress as possible. You can replicate this approach on your own. If you really want to kick your trolls in the teeth, create your own writing practice, set your word count goals (see Chapter 7), and set up your own writing community. It could be you and one other person, or it could be a group of people. This is not a critique group; it's people showing up for each other to help everyone in the group stay accountable to their goals.

If you'd like to join our writing sprint community, Top Three Authors' Club, we meet twice a day, Monday through Friday. This is not part of the workshop; it's simply a membership to help you stay accountable. I lead the group at least a couple of times each week, so it's also a great way to get some of your questions answered. For more information, visit ajharper.com.

It took me more than a decade to figure out that writer's block is not a thing, and a few more years to come up with a proven way to combat the thing that makes us feel as though it's real. A lot of things in life are possibly true and might work. This system, though, actually does work. I hope you'll give it a try for at least four weeks and find out for yourself.

You Have No Good Reason

The Sunday before the first day of Sprintapalooza, I called my Dean of Students, Laura Stone. I try not to bother her on weekends, but I had been head down, editing manuscripts for a couple of weeks, and I needed a quick chat about managing my time so I could finish edits on *this* book.

Before we signed off, Laura told me she planned to join the six a.m. sprints, which are five a.m. for her, and focus solely on her novel.

"No work tasks," she said. "I've been avoiding my book again, and I need to get back into it."

Laura had been working on her fourth novel for years. She'd set it aside for various reasons, some of them unavoidable, and some of them for the same reason we often set aside creative projects: Resistance gets the better of us. It happens to new authors and seasoned authors, to published and unpublished authors, to unknown authors and internationally famous authors. Resistance does not discriminate. The experience is so common, and yet, it's not common for Laura Stone. You see, she's an alien. She wrote the first draft of her third novel in eight days. She once turned in her copy edits in less than eight hours. Yeah, she's one of those weirdos. So the fact that she still had more than half of her novel to finish after years of working on it had caused her to question if she had a deeper problem.

Over the years, she'd told herself many things: the story was so dark, she needed a break from it; she didn't know enough about swamps yet; she should pull back and re-evaluate so she didn't end up writing "poverty porn." (Kinda makes you want to read it now, doesn't it?)

"I'm spending the day figuring out why I keep dropping this story. I want to understand why it's so hard for me to finish."

Oh no. Red flag.

After receiving her permission to offer her some advice, I said, "Laura, you know trying to understand why you're avoiding your novel is another form of Resistance."

Then she said, "It's just . . . I'm so sad. I need to spend time thinking about why this novel is making me sad."

She went on to tell me about her feelings. Convinced that her sadness had prevented her from finishing the book, she wanted to get at the reason behind it.

"There's no point in trying to get at the root of the problem," I said. "The cure is the same. The cure for the Resistance is the same. The cure for the sadness is the same. Show up to write."

The trolls are really, really good liars. Sometimes they are overtly nasty, telling us we suck and we'll never amount to anything. It's almost easier to deal with those trolls, because they are so freaking obvious. You can knock them off your desk and say, "Yeah, yeah. Get a new act."

It's the *reasonable* trolls that do the most damage. They sit on our shoulders and convince us there's a good reason to set our writing aside. The one that always gets me, even though I know the trap, is the troll who says, "Psst. You have other, more pressing work to do." Yup. Hard to argue with that one. It's true, and it really doesn't matter how much work I have to do. I can spare twenty minutes to write a few words and keep my book top of mind.

Here's some other Reasonable Shoulder Troll classics:

"You've worked so hard. You deserve a break."

"You need to focus on paying work."

"You can start again after you finish your research."

"You need to get organized first."

"You should get some feedback before you write any more, to make sure you're on the right track."

"Your kids need you."

"You should sleep in. You need your rest."

All good, reasonable reasons to set your book aside for the day. Except you end up doing that on most days. And eventually, the Reasonable Shoulder Troll convinces you to take a longer break from your book.

"You just need to clear the decks. You can start again in the fall when things calm down."

Yup. Makes sense.

And then, in the fall, the Reasonable Shoulder Troll goes in for the kill:

"You don't have to write this book, you know. You can let it go."

See, this is the troll that can make you give up, because there's always a grain of truth in everything it says. Yes, there are probably other worthwhile things you could or even should be doing. Sure, you can "let go." (Translation: give up.) No, you don't have to write your book. All those statements could be true.

And because all those statements could be true, it's so damn easy for you to quit.

Whenever you hear the Reasonable Shoulder Troll whisper in your ear in its soft, unassuming voice, I want you to remember that I told you that you have no good reason to stop working on your book. Even if something important comes up, you can still knock out twenty words. Or ten. Or even five. Just by attending to your book, in whatever small way, you beat the trolls for the day. We don't have to be great to beat them. We don't even have to be prolific to beat them. We just have to show up.

The cure is the same, no matter what problem you believe is at the source of your Resistance. Laura could spend days, weeks, maybe even years trying to figure out the cause of her sadness around writing her novel. It might seem like time well spent, but it's not. Because trying to dig up the root of the problem with our inability to put in ass in chair and get words on the page is its own form of Resistance.

You don't have to feel better to write.

You don't have to understand yourself better to write.

You don't have to conquer some other issue before you can write.

You don't have to be ready to write.

You don't have to feel inspired to write.

You just have to show up—and write.

Later that day, I noticed a post on Laura's social media accounts. It was a video of her whiteboard, on which she's been plotting her novel. In the morning, when we started Sprintapalooza, it was pretty much blank. After a day of writing sprints, she had two columns of content. When I unmuted the video, I heard the hard-driving sound of Aerosmith's "Back in the Saddle."

Yeah, you are, Laura.

Reader First Is a Troll-Killer

Want some good news about the trolls? You already have a terrific weapon in your troll-killer arsenal: Reader First. Whenever you're caught up in negative thoughts about your ability to write a must-read book, or any book, remind yourself that you are writing to serve your readers. Think about how you can help them. Think about what you need to tell them to help them feel better or to help them understand. Think about the people who would have better lives, better marriages, better businesses, better whatever you're promising because they read your book. Think about the people who *need* your book.

"The first draft is just math" is a pretty effective tool to hold back your army of trolls, but when they have you surrounded, think Reader First. This simple shift in perspective is your ultimate troll-killer. Yes, trolls are like zombies—they rise from the dead the next day. But you can strike them dead for a few hours when you stop thinking about *how* you're writing and start thinking about *who* you're writing for.

Here are some other helpful tools to beat your trolls.

If You're Stuck, Use Prompts

Back in my ghostwriting days, I often sent prompts to my clients to help them "download" information and stories from their brain that I could use to draft their manuscripts. I told them to answer the questions as if they were talking directly to their reader. When they felt stuck or overwhelmed with all the ideas and wisdom rolling around in their heads, the prompts helped them to free that content in an organized way.

If you're feeling especially stuck, look at your teaching points and come up with your own prompts. Then answer the questions as if you are speaking directly to your reader. You could have just a couple of questions per teaching point or several; there's no magic number.

Let's say you are stuck on how to write the teaching point "Stretch goals help you move faster toward your dreams." Draft a bunch of questions people have asked you—and those you've asked yourself—about stretch goals. For example:

- What is a stretch goal?
- What's the difference between a stretch goal and a small, achievable goal?
- How do I know if a stretch goal is really a stretch?
- How do I know if I've set a goal that stretches me too far?
- Should I only have stretch goals, or should I also have smaller goals?
- Should I only have one stretch goal at a time?

Now, if you really want to dazzle yourself with the content from your own brain, take these prompts to the next level with this simple addition to every question: "Can you give me an example?" This simple, yet powerful, question unlocks even more juicy info and is the key to finding analogies, anecdotes, and stories that help your reader understand and believe your teaching points.

Remember the interview questions from Chapter 5? You can use them on yourself:

"How do I know this to be true?"

"When did I learn this?"

You can also add these questions to your prompt list to dig up stories in your brain.

You'll need to edit your answers to create a section in your book, but it's much easier to do that than it is to face the blank page.

If You Can't Write, Talk

Once you have your prompts, you can try this other super-effective way to unblock yourself: record yourself answering the questions. Sometimes it's difficult just to face the page, so grab your phone or a voice recorder and your prompts, and just answer a few each day. You can do this on the couch, in your car, on a walk, or wherever you feel comfortable.

Then have the audio transcribed or do it yourself. The act of transcribing your own content can inspire further ideas. If you're not a fast typist and/or don't want to take the time, there are lots of free and low-cost transcription options for you. Sometimes the text isn't exactly right, so make sure you read through your transcription within a few days of recording it, while you remember what you meant to say. And move your transcription where it belongs in your manuscript. Just copy and paste it right into the doc. That way, you won't have to filter through it later. One more tip: Highlight the parts of the text that you think you're likely to use. You'll save yourself time later.

You might have heard of people "talking" their books. This only works well for a first draft, and it only works at all if you have an outline and prompts. It doesn't work if you just ramble on and tell yourself you'll figure it out later. Reader First. Answer their questions. Address their concerns. It's not about you.

What I Really Want to Write About Is...

Laura Stone shared a tool with me that she uses to get unstuck, and she gave me permission to share it with you. I've tried it, my students have tried it, and it works very well.

Consider one of your teaching points, or your Core Message, and then use this sentence to start writing: "What I really want to write about is . . ." Let yourself go as you fill in the blank. Write as little or as much as you want. You may discover a new story, or an idea about how you want to frame a teaching point. Or you may simply get past your block and feel inspired to keep writing. For me, it works like a charm.

I also like to use a variation of Laura's tool. I start writing with this sentence: "What I really *don't* want to write about is . . ." This is helpful when you are stuck in self-censor mode. Just spell out what you don't want to touch in your book. It could be that you are writing a story about your childhood and it includes some things that might upset your mom. Or it could be that you are writing a chapter about online marketing and you don't want to sound like every other guru on the planet. Writing about what you don't want to write about can help you get those feelings out so that you can write what you *do* want to write about. It can also help you clarify how you want to show up as an author. Give it a try.

Feedback Is the Troll's Playground

Writing can be a lonely endeavor. This is one of the reasons why in Top Three Book Workshop, we write together whenever possible. Writing in community helps us ignore that little nagging voice inside that keeps telling us that our ideas are not worth pursuing, that no one will read our books, or finish our books, or seek us out because of our books. That voice is loud throughout the entire process of writing and editing, and so we start to want feedback to see if we are on the right track. We think we need someone, anyone, to tell us if the book is any good.

Translation: We want them to tell us if *we* are any good.

I understand the urge to get someone to read our work at this stage. My advice about that is simple: Don't do it.

When you are in first-draft mode, you need to treat your book like a little baby. A baby you need to protect and keep safe. No germs. Cradle the head. Limit exposure to other people. Treat it with tender loving care. Don't hand your book baby off to someone who is not qualified to give you feedback, because that might derail your efforts. When your book baby is in the fragile, infant stage, you will naturally want reassurance that it's good. That you have something worth saying. That you're not wasting your time. Try to resist the urge to share your unfinished, unedited draft with others, including the people who love you and want you to succeed. Even the most well-intentioned people could end up saying something that stalls your efforts or sends you down a dead-end path.

Substantive/developmental editors can fulfill your need for feedback later in the process, after you've completed your first draft and some self-editing. They help you shape the book and make it better, and they will tell you when you are on the right track. (I'll share more about editors in Chapter 15.) And soon enough, you'll be ready to share your edited, in-progress manuscript with your advance readers. For now, resist the urge to say, "Can I show you something?" and hand over your precious infant. Give it time to grow and get stronger before you let it out in the world.

It's Not Zero

I've come to believe that the part of us that believes we can crank out a draft in record time is also a form of Resistance. We think of it as the thing that keeps us from facing the page, but I think banging out a first draft and then publishing in ninety days, or whatever number you choose, is resisting the true possibility of your idea, realized. Whether I'm right or wrong about that, breaking your project down into manageable, daily pieces is a much easier way to go about getting it done.

In the last chapter, I shared how my dad's approach to passing his CPA exam on the first try helped me come up with "the first draft is just math." I'd like to share another Dad-ism with you that I often say to my workshop authors to help them stay the course.

When I was a kid and lamented my haul at Halloween was less than I'd hoped it would be, Dad would say, "Well, it's not zero." As a new adult, when I complained about my nearly empty bank account, he'd say, "Well, it's not zero." And so on. His point was, any amount is better than zero. Now, when my authors apologize for or are ashamed to share their daily word count with our group, I say, "Well, it's not zero." A lower-than-you'd-hoped-to-write word count doesn't matter. What matters is, you wrote some words. Even a few words count. Even a couple. Even one word. They count because you showed up. You attended to your seedling. You kicked the trolls in the teeth that day. You didn't let them win.

Write for Inspiration

I'm an expert at relocating. By the time I was eighteen, I had already moved fifteen times. I don't remember the early moves, but the rest are imprinted on my mind. For most, Mom would rally her friends to help her and pay them in pizza and beer—standard operating procedure for most Midwestern folks.

Through all the moves, the one constant was The Great Agate—a rock about the size of a watermelon. No matter what else she got rid of, Mom always brought it with us. I can still remember her friends complaining about lifting that massive thing.

The Great Agate was tangible proof of one of the core family stories Mom told me. Growing up, her beloved father would take her and her siblings up to the North Shore of Lake Superior to hunt for agates.

Mom told the story like this: "All we wanted was to find a really big agate, but we only found tiny stones. We looked and looked, and grew frustrated. Then Dad said, 'The best way to find a big agate is to look for the little ones.' We didn't believe him at first, but we did as we were told. All day we looked for small agates and put them in our pockets. Then, when we were just about to call it a day, we found it—The Great Agate."

I'm pretty sure I heard that story about a dozen times growing up. Typically, she would share it when she wanted me to stay focused on the small goals to win the big prize, or something like that. The story, which now feels like a gift from my grandfather, really hit home when I made the connection between hunting for agates and writing practice. Rather than search (or worse, wait) for your big aha moment, the big burst of inspiration, the big money idea, focus on writing practice, and you'll find it.

We don't always want to do the grunt work, and we are often frustrated with what seems like slow progress when we write just a few hundred words a day. We book hotel rooms for the weekend, or longer, as self-imposed writing retreats and set unrealistic goals for ourselves. Don't get me wrong—I love a good writing retreat, especially in a hotel with room service, but going in with the expectation of writing an opus, or figuring out a major problem, or knocking out your whole book or even a few chapters only sets you up for disappointment. Every time I've booked a hotel room to write, I ended up spending half the time sleeping and another third watching reruns of *Law & Order*.

Rather than wait for inspiration to write, write for inspiration. Sit down and do the work, even when you don't feel like it. If you do this consistently at least five days a week, within two to three weeks you'll start to get regular "gifts"—ideas, fixes, connections.

It's the daily progress that begets the big ideas and aha moments. The pearls of wisdom. The Great Agates and the Holy Grails. Keep looking for the little ones and you'll find it.

Your Book in the Wild

It's time for you to come out of your cave and write with other people.[4] Again, you don't need more than one person, though a group is more fun—and better at holding you accountable. Follow the guidelines I shared in this chapter. When combined with regular writing practice and working toward a word count goal, writing sprints will ensure you knock out your first draft efficiently, so you can get to the real work: editing.

Onward!

---

4   You can join my sprint group, Top Three Authors' Club, at any time, and I have a pay-what-you-can option. If it fits your schedule and your budget, I hope to see you there. I'd love to hear about your book.

PART THREE

Edit

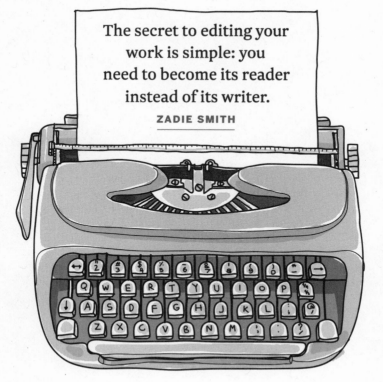

The secret to editing your work is simple: you need to become its reader instead of its writer.

ZADIE SMITH

The Must-Read
Editing Method

I T WAS my first proper ghostwriting job. I had been writing short ebooks for a few months, nothing over 25,000 words. This job, though—this was a legit book that would be on legit bookstore shelves. The author asked for a *"Sex and the City,* Carrie Bradshaw tone," and I knew I could pull that off. She's just a character, right? Sassy, strong, and full of heart. Can do!

For months, I pored over the pages of research the author sent and my own notes from our many phone interviews. I had sent her a few chapters during that time, which she loved, so I carried on. Then it came time to deliver the complete first draft. Not an SFD. It was my job to make sure I submitted a decent first draft. A good first draft. A first draft that had potential for greatness.

I couldn't do it.

I had this nagging feeling that I had missed something, that I'd screwed up, that the book was trash. So I let the deadline pass. And pass again. Each time I sat down at my computer to finish the last bits, I froze. A too-hot, panicky feeling enveloped me. Words swam on the page as I scrolled, and scrolled, and scrolled through the document, my cursor never landing. The keys on my keyboard seemed tiny and my fingers suddenly seemed too fat and heavy to type effectively.

This paralysis was not a new experience for me. Fear that I would turn in something less than stellar permeated my writing life from the time I was a teenager. Concern that I'd forgotten something important had been with me since I was a young child. I worried constantly—about everything. We didn't talk about anxiety in the eighties. I didn't know it was a thing, and few people discussed it with respect to children.

I had read about "editing passes," where you start at page one and work your way through the entire manuscript, but I had no idea how I could possibly check for everything I was worried about at the same time. What if the reader has a hard time understanding some of the concepts or teaching points? What if the reader feels overwhelmed by the content? What if the reader thinks the action steps are too hard? What if the reader gets bored (or angry, or frustrated) and gives up on the book?

Eventually, I pushed the deadline for the complete first draft so far back, I had no choice but to finish. Then I remembered how I coped with my fretting ways when I was a child: I made checklists.

- "Everything I Need to Do Before Summer Vacation"
- "Things to Clean Before Grandma Peg Visits"
- "Books I Must Read Before I Get a Mentor"

Notice the commonality. *Before.* Before you do anything, make sure you do all these other things. Lots to unpack there, but I didn't have the time to think about it. I had to deliver the manuscript and get paid. Were the lists compulsive? Yes. Did they help me calm down? Absolutely.

So I made another list. An editing checklist.

- "Editing Passes to Complete Before I Turn In the Manuscript."

I had to be sure that the book delivered—for the client and for the reader. Creating a checklist was the only way my compulsive mind could be sure that I had accomplished that goal.

That initial list looked something like this:

1 Stories: trim/unpack.
2 Flow/progression of thought.
3 Clarity.
4 Carrie Bradshaw.
5 Exercises doable?
6 Transitions.
7 Preachy?
8 Missing data?
9 Formatting.
10 Citations.

Once I'd jotted down everything I wanted to double-check, I went through the manuscript and addressed them one at a time. To be clear, this does not mean that I started with page one and read every single word for each task on my list. I knew where to look for the edits. For example, to work on my stories, all I had to do was turn to the stories and make sure I had unpacked the key moments and that I hadn't included too much exposition. When I checked the progression of thought, the flow of teaching points, I flipped through the book and looked at chapter and section titles to make sure I had sequenced the book in a way that would make sense to a reader. Addressing transitions required I look at the start and close of each chapter and section. As for the Carrie Bradshaw tone the client wanted, I tackled that with my final, page-one pass—when I read through the entire manuscript from page one until the final word.

After I finished my editing checklist, that nagging feeling that I had missed something disappeared and my anxiety about how the manuscript would be received dissipated significantly. I sent it off to my client with a feeling of pride.

Of course, we had much more editing to do, including editing you may already be familiar with, such as copy editing and proofreading. Still, I knew that I had done all I could to write the book my client wanted. More importantly, I had done my best to ensure the reader understood the teaching points, could actually *do* the exercises my client wanted them to do, and could achieve the outcomes my client promised.

I didn't realize until later that, due to my anxiety and compulsive thinking, I had created a method for editing books that ensured the reader could experience a real transformation, provided they finished the book and acted on the author's advice. Not just over time—but by the time they turned the very last page.

The Must-Read Editing Method[5] starts with the reader-focused checklist and ends with the page-one pass most writers and editors do. Each task on the checklist is its own pass, which allows you to focus on one issue at a time and make sure you've covered it. Then, when you do your final read-through, the page-one pass, you don't stop and start and scroll back and forward. You can read it all the way through. More importantly, you've edited with the intent to create a transformational experience for your reader.

Using the Must-Read Editing Method also makes the process easier and less nerve-racking. If you're like me and you worry that you'll miss something important, this approach will help you move forward with confidence. And if you're not like me and don't worry quite as much, this approach will help you move forward with confidence. That's right—either way, it's an editing system that works.

The Editing Pass Checklist I Use Today

My Editing Pass Checklist has evolved since that first book. I think about it in terms of different goals I want to achieve, and the passes I'll need to do to achieve those goals.

Here's the version I use today.

---

5   If you'd like to work with a Must-Read Editing Method certified developmental editor, or if you'd like to become certified and gain referrals for Top Three Book Workshop students, visit my website (ajharper.com/editors).

Goal: Reader Transformation

1 Mapping the Reader Journey
2 Core Message
3 Promise
4 Doability
5 Stories
6 Sequencing

Goal: Deep Reader Connection

7 Immutable Laws and Characteristics
8 Doubts, Objections, and Criticisms
9 Burning Questions and Chief Concerns
10 Diversity and Inclusiveness

Goal: Keep Your Reader on the Page

11 Clarity and Assumptions
12 Redundancies and Unintentional Repetitiveness
13 Accessibility and Learning Styles
14 Feedback Protocol
15 Sources and Citations
16 Submission Checklist

Goal: Revenue and Reader Engagement

17 Seeds for Next Steps

This is the same checklist I use for Mike Michalowicz's books, the same checklist I show my authors how to work through in workshop, and the same checklist I used for this book. You can download your own copy from the Must-Read website (writeamustread.com/tools). Or, if you want more guidance and need community and accountability, you may want to sign up for one of my six-week Must-Read Editing Workshops.

As I shared earlier, when you use the Must-Read Editing Method, editing passes are not complete reviews. They are tactical. Only the final, page-one pass is a full read-through. In the next five chapters, I'll explain each pass and give you some examples. Each of the chapters is a mega-workshop chapter because every single pass is an exercise that will take some time to get through. You may want to read through the chapters and get a feel for the checklist. Or you might read about one pass, do the pass, and move on. Up to you. Just—no matter what, don't give up. You'll get through it, and your book will be *so* much better because you did.

Other Book-Specific To-Dos

For each book, I usually have a few other passes I need to add to my list that I won't need with other books. For *Get Different*, I had to add a "Mike's audio texts" pass, because he had started sending me these audio texts with ideas and I wanted to make sure I'd handled them before we submitted. Sometimes I have a lot of content in the "Stuff I Did Not Use" Word file I create to dump deleted text, so I'll add a pass to review that doc and any other content files I gathered before and during the writing process. Sometimes I've written stories or case studies that are still evolving, so I add a "Results Update" pass and check in with people I've interviewed to see if they have new outcomes to share that would enhance their story and improve social proof. You may add a pass for words you overuse, so you can go back and fix them. (Try writing this book and limiting your use of the word "reader." Whew!) You may need to double-check statistics or other data to see if it's been updated during your writing and editing process.

Truly, anything you're worried about, make it a pass. Remember my story at the start of this chapter, about how my compulsive thinking helped me create this editing method? When you're concerned about some aspect of your book, just add it to the list and tell yourself you'll deal with it when you tackle editing passes. This allows you to move forward and keep writing.

A Quick Primer on the Editing Process

If you aren't sure what editing is, or the different types of editors you may encounter as an author, you are not alone. You aren't expected to know this right from the get-go, and many published authors still aren't sure what type of editing and editors they need. This is because traditional publishers can be tight-lipped about the process, and self-publishing companies (and some "experts"), in an effort to get books done fast and cheaply, often omit the most time-consuming—and super-important—phase of editing.

In Chapter 15, I give you a crash course in publishing so you can better understand the process and how to navigate it. For now, here's a brief rundown of the different types of editing, and in which order you need them.

Developmental. This is the person who helps you develop your concept, message, and transformational outline. They also help you with big-picture stuff to make sure you're on track before you write and as you are writing. When I work with authors in the first five weeks of workshop, this is developmental editing.

If you already have a traditional deal, the editor assigned to your book will serve in this capacity, if needed. This is a bit of a chicken-before-the-egg deal, because you need a stellar concept, message, and outline to *get* the deal in the first place, unless you're a celebrity or can otherwise prove you can sell an ass-ton of books. The way you demonstrate your concept is with a book proposal.

An important note: A developmental editor can also be your substantive editor (see below). These are different types of editing that are almost always handled by the same person. Why? Because developmental editors and substantive editors handle the big questions: Does your book work? Does it do the job you intended it to do? (Hello, Promise.) If you plan to self-publish and you followed the exercises in this book, you can skip working with a developmental editor before you start writing and work with a substantive editor after you have a first draft.

Self. Once you have a first draft, it's up to you to prepare it for submission to your editor, no matter which publishing path you choose. This is where the Must-Read Editing Method becomes your saving grace. Many authors aren't sure what's needed in this stage, so they tend to send their manuscripts to editors way before they're ready. This stage could take you two weeks, two months, or longer. It depends on the length of your book, how much you need to change, add, or fix, and how much time you have in your schedule to devote to your book.

By taking the time to do your self-edit, you will save yourself so much stress in the next stage, because your substantive editor won't have as much work to do. If you're self-publishing, this can also save you heaps of cash. The good news is, you are about to learn exactly how to self-edit your book so you don't have to wander around in the "woods" of your manuscript wondering "Where do I start?" and "How do I know what to fix?"

Substantive. After you've done all you can with your own edits, next you move to substantive editing. As noted above, this editor is the person who will help you make sure your book works, that it meets your vision, that it lives up to all it can be. A developmental editor is often also the substantive editor, and the terms are often used interchangeably. For the purposes of this book, a developmental editor comes in before you have a first draft, and a substantive editor comes in after you have a first draft.

When I work with authors in the last five weeks of workshop, this is substantive editing. I give them feedback on their first draft directed toward storytelling, flow, Reader Journey, clarity, and other key points. At this stage, we consider major questions such as: Does this structure work? Is the tone consistent and one that would appeal to readers? Is this content clear? Which content serves the reader and which does not? How can we simplify this? How can we simplify it even further? How can we simplify it yet again?

For most traditional publishing deals, you'll have an editor assigned to you for this purpose. You'll usually have two rounds of substantive editing—one where they give you an editorial letter (or email) with notes giving recommendations for improvements as well as your manuscript with specific comments. Once you've revised your manuscript based on their notes, they'll do a second round, line edits. This includes their edits of your text, as well as additional comments based on your revisions. They will also shepherd your book through the production process (more on that in Chapter 15).

Copy edit. Once your book is in good shape, you are ready for copy edit. You are not ready for copy edit if you still have big changes to make.

This is the stage of editing that most people think comes next after you turn in your first draft. Now you know better. Your copy editor will review your manuscript for grammar, punctuation, and formatting errors; inconsistencies; and syntax issues. They will also confirm some basics for you, such as the correct name of a company or the correct date of an event. It is not their job to check your non-English words, your scientific theories, or specific terms that would require, say, a medical textbook. Your copy editor may also point out some words or phrases that may be offensive to readers.

The copy editor is not also your developmental/substantive editor. This is because you need a different person for each stage of editing. Our brains fill in gaps and make simple corrections, and your developmental/substantive editor will surely miss stuff because they've already read your manuscript a few times. Also, developmental/substantive editors and copy editors do different things and require different training. (You do *not* want me to copy edit your book, and I wouldn't even try.)

The copy editing process can take four to eight weeks.

Proofread. After your book is typeset, and sometimes before, your next round of editing is proofreading. The proofreader checks for inconsistencies in text and formatting, as well as errors that may have been missed on previous passes, or that were created in typeset. Again, this is a different person for the reasons stated above. This is also when you read through your manuscript for the last time. This process could be as quick as one week, but it is more likely to take several weeks, including your review.

Your book deserves three qualified editors (developmental/substantive editor, copy editor, proofreader), so no matter which publishing path you choose, ensure you have all three. Your book also deserves the time to get it right, so allow more time than you think you'll need for each stage.

You may be wondering why I've asked you to take the time to self-edit your book. Wouldn't the editors handle it? Yes, you can rely on a good developmental/substantive editor to help you see gaps and opportunities, to refine your manuscript and make it better. Your copy editor will fix your grammar and errors and point out where you overuse words. However, editing is like renovating an overgrown garden. First you pull away the brush and debris so you can see the lay of the land. Only then can you start to envision a new space. You'll need more editing passes if your editors have to do a lot of the work that you *could* do. Not only does that add up in terms of cost and time, it also limits your editor's ability to do their best work for you. Don't send your editors a hot mess, okay? It's better for you and your reader if you do all you can and then send it along.

How Many Drafts Will You Need?

A few times a year, I host an intimate editing retreat for my Top Three Book Workshop alums. For three days, we go deep on four chapters of their book and apply the lessons of editing passes.

I recall at one retreat, Sue Barber, author of *The Visibility Factor*, asked me, "How many drafts should we expect to do?"

At the time, Sue had clocked several drafts of her first few chapters and hadn't begun to edit the back half of her book. I wish I could have given her a number. It could be ten drafts. Or twenty. Or somewhere in between. (Hopefully, it's not more than twenty, but that does happen.) You know you'll have a first draft. Your self-edit is a second draft—including all of the passes. You might set the manuscript aside for a bit to think through some things, or to test drive your content, and then edit it again later. That's a third draft. After you get back first-round notes from your developmental/substantive editor, you're working on your fourth draft. After line edits, number five. After Feedback Protocol, six. A page-one pass. Seven. The copy edited draft is eight, your revisions nine. Then finally, finally, you read through your first-pass pages, the typeset version of your book. If you decide to make a big change to your manuscript along the way, you could have a few more drafts somewhere in that sequence. Although I can't predict how many drafts you'll end up with at the end of your process, I do know it will be way more than you think.

Growing up one of my favorite movies was *Terms of Endearment*. My BFF Stacie and I watched it over and over again. Why we wanted to watch a mother-daughter drama in which the daughter dies of cancer I have no idea, but we must have seen it twenty times before we were fifteen.

In the movie, Debra Winger, who plays Emma, has a talk with her estranged husband about who should raise their kids—him, or her mother. Debra has a line about parenting that has stayed with me all these years: "As hard as you think it's going to be, you end up wishing it were that easy."

So true about parenting. And I think it applies to editing your book. (Actually, it applies to every stage of authorship.) As hard as you think it will be, you end up wishing it were that easy. You may tell yourself, "I can't handle eleven drafts. I'll lose my mind." And in the end, you may surpass that number and say, "Eleven drafts! That's nothing!"

I don't want to freak you out, but there's no point in withholding the truth from you. Maybe you'll knock it out in just a few drafts. Some of my authors have done that. Others have needed a few more.

At one point in her editing journey, Sue said, "I'm not sure I can do this. I'm not sure I can actually produce the book I want to give to readers."

Sue wanted her readers to feel like she was their coach. She wanted them to feel the way her clients feel when they are in a session with her. She wanted to provide them with a practical approach, but also so much heart and vulnerability. This last part did not come naturally to her, and I pushed her to dig deep and send me another draft. And another. To her credit, Sue stayed in it. She probably lost count of her drafts. (I know I don't count them.) She simply kept at it and stayed focused on her reader. That's what you need to remember to do, too. Your goal is to be in service to your reader and write the book you intended to write, not to "get it out in time for Christmas."

There's lovely postscript to Sue's story.

I encourage my authors to submit their books for trade review. This is a professional, critical review as opposed to a reader review. Trade reviews are published in journals such as *Publishers Weekly*, *Kirkus*, and *Foreword*, to name a few, and help authors get exposure to book buyers, librarians, and other industry professionals.

When her first trade review came back from *Publishers Weekly's BookLife*, I cried. Yes, real tears. Here's the line that did it:

"She writes as an engaged, encouraging coach..."

Not only did Sue achieve her goal; the professional reviewer saw it and commented on it—in a review that has a word count limit!

Mission accomplished. Know why?

Edits.

I loved the part of the review that called her book a "polished and practical guide."

Polished. Yup. Know why?

Edits.

Sue went on to get rave reviews from other trade journals, including the toughest of all, *Kirkus*. Here's a pull quote from that review that caught my eye, because I had heard Sue mention many times that she wasn't sure how to handle the storytelling, which is probably one of the most common concerns my authors have.

> *Barber smoothly weaves together stories from her own experience and case studies from coaching clients and co-workers she's known, relating a wide variety of scenarios involving workers in various capacities whose self-doubt or lack of clarity kept them in the "shadows," and lacking the confidence to realize their own power.*

Sue. My dear Sue. You did it. You freaking did it.

You can, too, you know. You can write the book you want to write, that makes the reader feel the way you want them to feel. You can write a book that critics "get" and appreciate, and readers love and talk about.

Know how you'll pull it off?

Edits.

As hard as you think it will be, you'll end up wishing it were that easy—and you'll be so glad you did it.

Your book is forever. Take the time to make it great.

The Odds Are in Your Favor

In my more than thirty years as a professional writer and seventeen years as a ghostwriter and editor, I have figured out the single most important factor in success as an author: persistence. The authors who show up day after day, who keep at it, almost always achieve success beyond their goals. The thing is, most people give up.

I remember a conversation I had with my mother when I was just a girl with a wish to be a writer. Even at the age of thirteen, I was down on myself, ready to set my dream aside, because I believed the hype about "the long shot." *Everyone wants to be a writer—what makes you think you can make a career out of that? It's really hard to get published. It's really hard to get noticed. The field is too crowded.*

In my mom's battered silver Honda, waiting for the engine to warm up, I slouched in my seat and stared at the defrost climbing up the window. Mom would always say, "When it looks like the shape of Batman, we can go." We were at the "two round-ish blobs" stage, no superhero in sight.

"People say the odds are one in a million," I said as I rubbed my gloved hands together. We hadn't had above-zero temps in weeks.

"Maybe they are," she replied. "But let's do the math. If one million people want to be a professional writer, at least half of them will never even start. They'll talk about it, but they won't write the first word. Another quarter will quit before they finish. Writing is hard, and most people get frustrated and give up. So now you have about two hundred and fifty thousand people."

"That's still a lot of people to compete with."

"True. But writers deal with a lot of rejection. At least another hundred and fifty thousand will throw in the towel at some point, because they'll think that it's hopeless. Or because they think that the decision-makers don't know what they're doing. Or because they believe their families when they tell them they should get a 'real job.' So now you have about one hundred thousand people vying for the same dream."

She let me sit quietly and think about those numbers. One hundred thousand people still seemed like an impossible number. It might as well have been a million.

As the bulbous shapes started to form Batman's wings, Mom said, "This is where craft makes the difference. Of the one hundred thousand people, at least half of them are not committed to craft, to learning how to get better, to listening to mentors and editors. They will only go so far because they think that they don't need any help. Now you have about fifty thousand people who are still in it with you."

I sat up taller in my seat.

"Of those fifty thousand," she continued, "only about ten thousand will have natural talent to do big things. So now you're one of ten thousand. What's left is luck, and you can beat those odds, too."

Mom switched from defrost to heat and the warm, dry air blasted my face. She put the car in reverse, and added, "You know how you can beat the odds, Annie? You beat the odds by trying. The more often you try, the more often you put yourself out there, the better your odds."

Suddenly my dream of becoming a successful writer seemed possible. Ten thousand was a lot of people, but nowhere near one million. I could work hard. I could get better. I could keep showing up. I had a chance.

You have a chance, too. In fact, the odds are better for you. Know why? Because your book can be one of many on the same topic. People don't read one book in your genre or with your focus and then stop. They read several books on your topic. Or maybe even hundreds of books on your topic. Sometimes people read several books with the same *message*.

Now, I know that my mother made up those numbers; she wasn't using exact science. But she wasn't far off. In my experience, many people who want to be authors don't start and most do give up before they finish, or too soon. Mom was being generous, because actually, that's almost everyone. Just by showing up every day, writing your book, getting better, continuing to grow as a writer, showing up for your readers in every way, you will get there. I know this for sure. I've seen it happen to people who absolutely deserved it and to people who were not pure of heart and probably didn't. The key differentiator for success is persistence. Just don't give up, and the odds are most definitely in your favor.

Your Book in the Wild

Okay, look—I'm willing to bet my original *Purple Rain* album that you haven't been celebrating your author milestones. Maybe it's because you aren't sure when reaching a milestone is a big deal.

Hear me now: Every milestone is a big deal.

If you've finished your first draft and you are ready to dig in to edits, time to break out the champagne. Get yourself a cake and ask the bakery to write "Congrats on Finishing Your First Draft." Take yourself out to dinner and tell your server it's a special occasion. However you choose to pat yourself on the back, document it and share it with the world. (And with me. Don't forget the #WriteAMustRead hashtag, so I can find your posts.) Starting edits is a major step on this wondrous/hellacious journey, and you deserve some props.

Onward!

CLAIM YOUR REWARD

After you've completed your super-rough draft, you'll need something super-special. Go to the Must-Read website (writeamustread .com/rewards) to unlock your prize.

Edit for Reader Transformation

"YOU ARE GOING to get so sick of hearing me say 'Reader First.' I keep saying it because you will forget."

This is my warning the first day of Top Three Book Workshop. And it's the reason why these first few editing passes are so important. No matter how committed you are to this approach to writing a must-read book, you will forget about your reader. It's not a character flaw; it's human. We get wrapped up in our own stuff. In completing the first draft, we shift from thinking about what the reader needs to trying to remember our stories, to explain our teaching points, to find our research. And we fight off an army of trolls every damn day. It's no wonder we need to be reminded that we are not assembling a collection of knowledge and stories. We are facilitating transformation.

A book is not about something. A book is for someone.

The first few editing passes are designed to ensure you deliver on the Promise, that you get your reader from where they are on page one to where you want them to be when they finish the book. To do that, we come back to Reader First. What needs to change in your manuscript to help the reader understand, believe, try, accept, do, learn, and push on?

As a reminder, I documented my process in creating this book for you on video, using screen share. You can see me complete each workshop section in my Behind the Book video series, which is free to download from my website (writeamustread.com/behindthebook).

Pass #1. Mapping the Reader Journey

Perhaps the most powerful editing tool I've developed, Mapping the Reader Journey is my very first pass because it often reveals necessary changes that may affect the structure of the book, such as gaps in content. In putting your reader first during the editing process, your primary objective is to ensure they have a transformational experience. When you outlined your book, you thought about what your reader needs first, next, and next. You thought about the Hero's Journey and how it connects to your reader's quest to reach your "Promiseland." Now, through Mapping the Reader Journey, you make sure that you're aware of what your reader thinks, feels, and understands as they read your content for the very first time.

1   **You are here.** Begin right at page one of your book, the starting point of the Reader Journey, and answer the following questions:

- What does your reader believe about your topic?

- What do they want and what do they perceive is standing in their way of them getting it? (Yes, I know you answered this in Chapter 2. We're circling back for a reason—to make sure we track the Reader Journey.)

- How confident do they feel that they can get what they want?

- What is your Promise to your reader?

- What mindset shift does your reader have to make in order for them to achieve that Promise?

2   **The destination.** Now fast-forward to the end of the book and answer the following questions:

- How have your reader's beliefs about your topic changed?

- Have you fulfilled your Promise to the reader?

- What is their "after"? How is their life/work/body/relationship different now, after reading your book?

- Is this the outcome you hoped to provide for your reader? If not, what do you need to change to get them there?

3   **The journey.** Here's the time-consuming part of this exercise. For each chapter, fill in the blanks. Now that they've read this chapter...

- My reader understands...

- My reader feels...

- My reader feels capable of doing...

- My reader is worried about...

- My reader still doesn't trust that...

- My reader is hitting the following roadblocks...

- My reader finds it easier to...

- My reader is becoming more...

- Is this where I want my reader to be right now? And if not, what do I need to change to fix that?

- How can I help my reader with any issues they may be having, as noted above?

I've noticed that some of my authors complete this exercise thinking about what they want for the reader, not thinking about their actual content and how it impacts the reader. The objective is to put yourself in your Ideal Reader's shoes and imagine how they experience your content *as it is right now*, not where you hope it will be when you're finished. When done right, this is an illuminating exercise that will help you see where you may need to make big and small changes to facilitate your reader's transformation.

Mapping the Reader Journey takes time. You may not be able to finish it in one sitting. You may also be tempted to ditch this step and get on with your other edits. Please hang in there and finish this editing pass. The insights you'll gain from this process will help you serve your reader and create a remarkable experience for them. This is the work. This is the craft in creating something truly transformational.

Pass #2. Core Message

For this second pass, I make sure that I've shared the Core Message throughout the book, not just in the introduction and first chapter. Sometimes we forget to remind our readers of our foundational truth because we are focused on writing the rest of our content. Intentional repetition shows the reader that *this is an important point.*

Start by searching for the exact wording of your Core Message. How many instances can you find? You may be surprised to discover you didn't mention it more than two or three times. We know it so well, and really, the whole book is about that message, so we think we're mentioning it all the time.

While writing this book, I also wrote another book with Mike Michalowicz, *Get Different: Marketing That Can't Be Ignored!* As I ran through my Editing Pass Checklist, I noticed we had only referenced the exact Core Message three times in the entire manuscript. Hitting the "next" button in the Find window, I kept expecting it to show up. *I'll find a couple of references in Chapter 4. That whole chapter is about how to be different.* Nope. *Okay, it's got to be in Chapter 7, where we run through the entire worksheet.* Nada. Nothing. Wow. We didn't even call back to the Core Message in the rally conclusion? *That's embarrassing.* I found variations on the Core Message, but not the exact wording, which is important when you close a book.

It's a bit tricky with this one, because like *Profit First*, the title *is* the Core Message, condensed. So references to the title of the book and to Get Different coaching and the branded worksheets made it seem as though we were constantly sharing the Core Message. In a way, we were, but was it enough? Remember, you want your reader to be able to tell people about your book, and that includes sharing the Core Message enough for them to remember it, but not so much that they want to smack you.

I made a point to go through and look for other places where inserting the Core Message would be helpful to the reader. For example, if I think the reader may need some encouragement to help get them out of their comfort zone, I could add it to remind them it's not just okay to be different; it's essential.

After you search for the exact wording of your Core Message, consider where else you could share it. You don't want to sprinkle it around like confetti. Look for places where it makes sense to call back to it. Where does your reader need to be reminded of that key point? Perhaps when they may be letting doubts get the better of them, or when they question if they can pull off this thing you're asking them to do. Maybe when they need to remember the transformational power of that statement, even if they remember nothing else.

Pass #3. Promise

Just as we forget to carry our Core Message through the book, we often forget to talk about the Promise. This pass requires looking for places where you could not only remind the reader of your Promise to them, but also show them how you have fulfilled it.

Let's say you've committed to this: "By the end of this book, you will feel a new sense of calm and you will have a set of tools to manage your stress so you can access that feeling at any time." Think about where in the Reader Journey they will start to feel calmer, and point it out. Reaching "Promiseland" is a collaboration between you and the reader. Highlight their progress. And remember, you can play with the Promise and rearrange the words.

So, for example, you might insert a reminder about how close the reader is to achieving the Promise of your book before or after the start of a new action step: "You've already filled your toolbox with seven techniques for managing stress. You are well on your way to feeling a new sense of calm."

Or you could kick off a midpoint chapter with a recap of all that the reader is now capable of doing: "Before we dive into this chapter, I want to honor you and your commitment to this process. Because you have stayed the course, read every page, and completed every exercise, you now have the ability to manage your stress and access a feeling of calm at any time. When you opened this book, you may not have thought it possible to have this power over your own mind, but you do. The rest of this journey will cement your knowledge and strengthen all you've gained."

Or you might perform a surgical edit after a story or case study, adding something like this: "Do you see how Anu was able to use her tools to step outside of a stressful situation and access a calm feeling, even though chaos whirled around her? That ability is yours if you simply practice these tools."

Pass #4. Doability

I'm a big fan of *The Great British Baking Show*. If you haven't seen it, in each episode, home bakers compete in three different challenges. The second is called "the technical," and it involves following a recipe they've never seen before, often for a type of baked good they've never heard of, much less eaten. To make it extra challenging, the recipes are pared down from what you'd find in a cookbook or online. For example, the instructions might say, "Make the dough," but not include any clues as to how long to knead it. Or they might say, "Bake," and not say how high the temperature should be or for how long. Super helpful, right? Holding back key information makes for good television, but how many contestants get the recipe right? Very few, if any. For most of them, it's a disaster. They struggle. They're confused. They make critical errors. And you know what they almost always end up saying about that recipe? "I'll never try this again."

This is what happens when we give our readers something to do that is not actually doable or is not a reasonable ask. Remember, they don't have your experience or depth of knowledge. They may have never seen or heard of your "recipe" before. And even if they could pull it off, is it too much to ask?

To make sure your asks are doable, follow these steps:

- This may seem like a no-brainer, but have you actually tried to do what you're asking your readers to do? You create tasks, maybe worksheets, maybe steps to follow, but have you tried to work through them from start to finish? If you get tripped up, expect your reader to have an even harder time of it. If it takes you longer than you thought to finish the task, your reader may need double or even triple that time.

- You know your reader. How much time do they have to devote to your "action steps"? What about resources? Do they have access to everything you say they need? Make the action easier on all fronts. Do they really have to do the entire exercise or task to make progress, or can they do a modified version? How could you tweak your ask so they don't have to buy anything or talk to an expert to complete it?

- If an action step requires some time, make that clear in your instructions. Again, you're managing expectations so your reader doesn't get frustrated with themselves and, consequently, with you. Nearly everything I've asked you to do in this book is pretty dang time-consuming. I mean, we're writing a must-read here, not a better business card. I've told you the exercises and editing passes I've asked you to do will take a while, though. I've bugged you about it incessantly. You know what you're getting into, and so when it takes time, you're not surprised. I've also told you that your first draft will suck, so right away I've taken the pressure off. Do the same for your reader, so they can do all the things you need them to do.

In this editing pass, you may discover that you need to ditch one or more of your action steps completely. That's okay. Reader first, last, and always!

Pass #5. Stories

The stories pass is a two-parter. First go through your teaching points and determine if you need more stories to help you clarify a teaching point, to connect with your reader, or to provide social proof. Look at your notes for the Mapping the Reader Journey pass, the first one on the checklist. There you will find places in your manuscript where you may need a story to help your reader process information, or feel better, or gather the courage to carry on.

The second part of this editing pass is improving those stories. Becoming a better storyteller is a lifelong endeavor. I've been at it since I was a kid hacking away on the electric Smith Corona typewriter my mom bought me for my birthday (best present ever). I try to get a little better at it every year, with every story. For this pass, I want you to go back over your stories and make them just a little bit better. Do you have too much exposition, otherwise known as setup? Do you tell us what happened when you could show us instead? Do your stories have a narrative arc and stakes, as you learned in Chapter 5? (For help editing stories, go to writeamustread.com/behindthebook.)

When I edit for my authors, I find they often have moments in stories or anecdotes that need to be unpacked. Just as we drive right by the scenic overlook in an effort to get where we're going, we sometimes forget to slow down for an important moment in a story.

I'll give you an example. Indrani Goradia is writing for people who have survived or are living with domestic violence. Her book is a message-based memoir of her early life in Trinidad, immigrating to the US, and coming to terms with the effects of abuse in her own life so she could save her children and save herself.

While at a Developmental Editing Retreat, Indrani read aloud from a story she had written about confronting her mother about the abuse. In that brief scene, she wrote one line that stood out like a neon sign against a black sky: "Her wrath no longer affected me."

Six words. In those six words she'd buried a deeper story that I knew she had to unpack. The entire book is Indrani's journey to get to that place of calm, and yet she had "driven" right past it. So I asked her to unpack her "six-word story." Show us more. Show us your feelings. Show us the conversation. Show us how your body reacts. Show us how your mother responds to your strength. *Show us.*

Why does it matter that Indrani unpack these specific six words?

Because her book is not about something. Her book is *for* someone.

Her book is not about domestic violence. Her book is for people who survived it and people who are living with it.

And those people, her "someones," need to see her *win.*

"Her wrath no longer affected me." That's the win for her, and the win her readers want, so she must unpack it. She must show them what is possible. She must show them the Promise.

Pass #6. Sequencing

Even if you carefully planned each chapter, you will undoubtedly still have sequencing issues when it comes to edit your draft. In Chapter 6 you learned about the Progression of Thought, the way your information unfolds to help your reader understand the information you present. Now that you have the words down, does the sequence still work? Do you have to move some things around for better flow?

In this pass, you are coming back to the goal of the outline: what your reader needs first, then next, then next, then next. In what order do they need your teaching points to unfold? You will likely move some chapters around. You may discover you need to break up chapters, or that you missed one entirely. For example, in editing her must-read book *Motherhood, Apple Pie, and All That Happy Horseshit,* Cyndi Thomason decided to expand her section on Sacred Space into its own chapter. Her book is for moms who own a business or want to start one, and also want to ensure it supports their personal values about family. She realized by fleshing it out and moving it up in the sequence, she would elevate the importance of the concept and provide her reader with an essential tool to do the reflective work that followed.

Sequencing is an art. I happen to have a knack for it, as do most developmental/substantive editors. Put yourself in your reader's shoes, and if you're still stuck on this pass, note that for your editor and move on. They will help you fix the order, if needed.

Your Book in the Wild

To help you stay the course, ask for some accountability. Download the Must-Read Editing Method "gold star" worksheet from the Must-Read website (writeamustread.com/tools). Snap a pic of it when you start and share it as a behind-the-scenes author moment. If you want me to see it, tag it with #WriteAMustRead. As you make progress, continue to post the sheet. This may seem like a silly thing to do, but man, if you've made it this far in the writing process, you damn well deserve some gold stars. And it's a great way to let your friends, family, and colleagues help you stay accountable to the process.

Onward!

Edit for Deep
Reader Connection

B Y NOW you know one of your prime objectives is to connect with your reader. Remember the second step in the Reader Transformation Sequence: Readers will read your book because you see them and you get them. I see authors work hard to establish a connection in the first few pages, and then lose it by Chapter 2 because they forgot to keep it going.

You see, it's easy to lose your reader along the way. They might disconnect from you if your tone changes, or if you offend them in some way. You could lose them if they feel you haven't addressed their issues. They'll hold out for a chapter or two, but if you never get to their questions and concerns, your reader will put the book down. And if you forget what it's like to work through this stuff—because you're past it, or because you've never had to deal with it yourself—that precious connection may break and they'll give up on your book entirely.

The next few passes will help you establish and keep a deep connection with your reader throughout your book, so much so that they will wonder how you know them so well.

Pass #7. Immutable Laws and Characteristics

Immutable Laws and Characteristics are the standards and qualities (tone) you set for each book.

This is the list you come up with when you complete the phrase "My book must always . . ."

Here are some examples:

"My book must always feel like a tough-love talk from an ass-kicking coach."

"My book must always feel like a warm hug from someone who loves you."

"My book must always be actionable and doable."

"My book must always make people feel hope for the future."

"My book must always be accessible. No guru- or professor-speak."

In her list of Immutable Laws and Characteristics, Top Three Book Workshop alum Gena Cox came up with "supportive, but provocative." A supportive tone is a differentiator for Gena's book in her genre. More importantly, it is in keeping with her values. Look up her book, *Leading Inclusion: Drive Change Your Employees Can See and Feel,* and you'll see that "supportive, but provocative" tone even influenced her cover! After you determine your book's Immutable Laws and Characteristics, your task is to make sure your book actually lived up to your list. Did you consistently hit the right tone? We tend to forget tone when we walk readers through complicated steps, for example, or present research. Sometimes we unknowingly fall back on the formality we learned to adopt in academia or business. Does your manuscript meet your standards? Does it represent you and your values in the way you intended?

Tweak your manuscript to fit your Immutable Laws and Characteristics. Sometimes authors want to address tone in the first draft. This is not a first-draft exercise. It takes practice—and edits—to ensure your voice is consistent throughout your manuscript. And in my experience, it's in writing your first draft that you *find* your voice. Kasey Compton is a great example of this. While writing her first book, *Fix This Next for Healthcare Providers,* she cruised through most of her book writing in an engaging, conversational style. When it came time to write her Call to Greatness, suddenly, there it was: her author voice. I give editorial feedback for my authors when they are in workshop, and I still remember my loud gasp when I read it the first time. She had written about her Grandma Lillie with such frank southern charm, I started calling her the "Fannie Flagg of business authors." (If you don't know Fannie Flagg, she wrote many wonderful novels, and her most famous of those is *Fried Green Tomatoes at the Whistle Stop Cafe*, which became a movie.) Finding her voice at the eleventh hour was a turning point for Kasey. Now, all she wants to do is write books. And with good reason—she's brilliant at it.

Pass #8. Doubts, Objections, and Criticisms

Here's one sure way to lose your reader: ignore their potential doubts, objections, and criticisms. As they read or listen, they process the words through the filter of their own opinions and experience; they won't take your advice and insights as absolutes or facts. Remember, your reader wants your book to be *the one*, and yet they come to the first page with a mixture of hope and skepticism. The skepticism is in part due to feeling shortchanged by other authors, but really, it's mostly about their own self-doubt.

You've experienced this; I'm certain of it. An author makes bold claims, shows you the way forward, and while some part of you wants to believe that they are right and everything they promise is possible, another part of you worries that their message, advice, process, or whatever won't work for you. When this feeling persists, you start to question whether the book has any value for you. If this feeling wins, you put the book down unfinished. Or you don't take action on anything you've learned.

Self-doubt bubbles up throughout the Reader Journey, and if you don't attend to it on the page, you may lose them. Criticism is often rooted in self-doubt. If a reader thinks they can't do something you've advocated, that can morph into judgment about your message, and about you. They don't trust you. They don't agree with you. And they don't like you.

Sometimes a reader's objections may require you to look at your own biases. It's important to consider that what is easy for you to implement may not be easy for your reader. A host of issues can impact their ability to pull something off—financial constraints, lack of time, mental health, lack of a strong support system, to name a few. The reader may think, "You don't know my life," and you don't. That said, you can show that you are aware that what is easy for you, or for someone else, may be a real challenge for others. Remember, some limitations are real and some are perceived, and it's not up to you to decide which is which.

You aren't going to connect with readers if you're the guru who doesn't consider how hard it is to do some of this stuff or how uncomfortable it can be to make a change. Think of your reader's insecurities like a leaky roof. If you ignore them too long, eventually your whole roof will cave in. They put the book down and never come back to it. They might even leave you a bad review. Most won't, though. The people who feel let down by your book will just put it down and not pick it up again. Then, when they're at a party or a conference, they may end up having an exchange like this this.

Random person: "Did you read that book 'such and such' by 'so-and-so'?"

Your reader: "Yeah. I just couldn't get through it. It's not really practical for real life."

As Scooby-Doo would say, "Ruh-roh." Now you have *negative* word of mouth about your book, and you don't even know it's happening. You can't see it or hear it, and you can't do anything about it.

While you can't account for each and every reason a reader may doubt or object to your content, you can show that you see them and you get them by performing surgical edits to address those doubts and objections.

Before you start this pass, make a list of potential doubts, objections, and criticisms your reader may have about your content. Here are some examples:

- This strategy won't work for me because . . .

- This process is too hard.

- This solution is too easy.

- No one else does it this way.

- I already tried this and it didn't work.

- Easy for you to say, with your [privilege, money, education, experience, support, courage, connections].

- I'll never convince my [spouse, family, kids, colleagues, staff, business partner, friends, community] to go along with this.

- What you're saying goes against everything I learned [in college, at work, from my parents, in my church, from my coach, from other authors/thought leaders].

- I'm not [smart, talented, educated, strong, young, old, fit, financially stable, experienced, beautiful, healthy, creative, brave] enough to pull this off.

Once you have a good list of doubts, objections, and criticisms, look through your manuscript and consider where some of these issues may come up for readers. You may have to go chapter by chapter. Then get in front of it. Name the doubt and address it in some fashion. If your process has time-consuming components (like this Must-Read Editing Pass Checklist!), you may need to get in front of your reader's worries to convince them that it's worth doing, despite the time investment. If your reader questions if something you advocate will work or not, you may need to add another results-oriented story or anecdote for social proof. If your Core Message is particularly controversial, you may need to address the fact that readers would likely have heard a very different message growing up.

Sometimes when you brainstorm the way your reader may be thinking or feeling, you end up hitting on one of your own insecurities. In one of my Developmental Editing Retreats, Dr. Gayle Friend, author of the forthcoming book *Trust Love Again*, did this exercise and then shared this reader criticism: "This stuff is too woo-woo." In her book, she offers profound techniques for improving intimacy in romantic relationships.

"Some of my techniques *are* pretty woo-woo," Gayle said. "I have one on love breathing, which is really important and helpful, but I worry that some people won't take it seriously, or take *me* seriously."

"Own the woo-woo," I said. "Lean into it. Don't try to hide it from readers or pretend it's not happening. You could say something like, 'I know this exercise may seem woo-woo to some of you. Guess what? It is. And guess what else? It works. And guess what *else*? You won't die. You'll make it through.' Or your version of that, Gayle."

In her solo edit work after that group session, she came back and shared two simple sentences she added to the intro to her "love breathing" exercise to get in front of the objection.

"Before your eyes glaze over because you think this is too woo-woo, remember that to breathe is to be alive. You can use breath to build resiliency and relax—or if you desire—to ignite passion."

Do you see how Gayle stuck in a pin in any potential objections to the exercise? You can make light of it and say, "Fight me!" or "Humor me." You can be encouraging and say, "Hang in there." You can be strong and say, "Just do it!" You can be bold and say, "What if you're wrong? What if I'm right?" What's the best approach for your reader? Funny? Heartfelt? Tough love? Remember, you don't have to write a soliloquy here. Surgical edits, my friend. Surgical edits.

This pass is one of the most important passes you'll do, because it helps the reader continue to feel seen and understood. You end up with reviews that include statements like, "I felt like the author read my mind." Yup. Because you thought about the experience of reading your book. Not such a revolutionary concept, I know. It's pretty basic. And yet, most authors don't do it. *You* are doing it, though. You care about your reader enough to consider them. You are willing to edit your manuscript so that they stay in it, so they feel empowered and keep pushing through, even if it's hard. You are determined to get them where they want to go and put the time in to make that happen.

Pass #9. Burning Questions and Chief Concerns

Remember I told you that you'd return to your Reader Profile again and again? This is one of those times. The good news is, this is an easy pass. Go back to your list of burning questions and chief concerns and ask yourself, "Have I answered each question? Have I addressed each concern?" If the answer is yes, move on. If you forgot about one of them, first determine if it still matters. Sometimes we come up with questions or concerns in the beginning of our development process that end up not being much of an issue after all, so why bother? If you do want to address a question or concern you inadvertently left out, where could you weave it in to enhance an existing section? Or do you need to create an entirely new section to cover it?

Pass #10. Diversity and Inclusiveness

I hope you have a lot of readers for your book and I hope those readers feel included in the important conversation you're having with the world. Language is powerful—it can make people feel welcome, and it can make people feel excluded. You may not mean to exclude a reader with your language, and I know you don't want to offend them. Still, sometimes our own biases get in the way and we inadvertently hurt readers with our words.

Here are some things to consider for this editing pass:

- **Representation.** Simply put, are most of your stories about people of the same race? Same religion? Same orientation? Same income level? Same ability? How could you diversify your stories, anecdotes, and case studies? In your fictional scenarios, do you use the same type of names?

- **Cultural appropriation.** Are you using phrases or slang words that have been appropriated from a culture that is not your own? If so, find another way to say it. A big one is "tribe." I'm sure I've used it in many books over the years, but once I learned that it is not appropriate for me, a non-Indigenous person, to use it, I stopped. It's a good word. I get it. But I promise there are other words you can use. Who knows? Maybe you'll coin a new term that we all end up using and crediting to you.

- **Hurtful words.** The list of words we use in everyday life that originated as slurs or were demeaning in some way is very, very long. I grew up in the eighties and I'm still working to unlearn a lot of then-socially-acceptable phrases that became part of my vocabulary. I'm including one here as a point of reference, and my deepest apologies to anyone who may be hurt by it. I've probably used the word "dumb" a thousand times in books. Then I learned that it was once a slur used against Deaf people. So not okay. I still have to catch myself sometimes. I'm working on it.

- **Sensitivity.** Sometimes you write something that is unintentionally insensitive. We all walk through life differently. For example, in *Get Different*, Mike tells a joke about being pulled over by the police. We edited that joke to acknowledge that some readers may not have the same thoughts running their heads when they imagine police sirens and flashing lights.

I strongly encourage you to take some sort of diversity and inclusion training. You may also want to work with an editor who is trained to be a sensitivity reader. That's not needed for most nonfiction books, but it can be super affordable and worth looking into.

Your Book in the Wild

As you work through the editing passes, you may come across a line or two you're confident will resonate with your Ideal Reader, lines you think they may save and quote when they read your book. Grab those lines and start using them on your website, on your social media, in emails—you know the drill by now. Start to build that connection now.
Onward!

Edit to Keep Your Reader on the Page

IN HIS BESTSELLING book *Friction: The Untapped Force That Can Be Your Most Powerful Advantage,* Roger Dooley explains friction as "the unnecessary expenditure of time, effort, or money in performing a task." He points out that $4.6 trillion of merchandise is left in abandoned e-commerce shopping carts and asserts that friction in purchasing is part of the reason why. I assert that friction in the reading experience is the main cause of book abandonment.

I searched high and low for statistics about how many people actually finish books, and came up empty. But you only have to look at your own pile of unfinished books to get a clue about that. Sure, there are many perfectly reasonable reasons why a person might set a book down—hurricane, fire, zombie apocalypse. But to not pick it back up again? Well, that book wasn't much of a page-turner, was it? What we're going for is a must-read, a book people can't wait to get back to after they escape the zombies. And to accomplish that goal, we need to remove as much friction as possible to create an immersive reading experience. In other words, we need to keep the reader on the page.

Most of my Editing Pass Checklist is about ensuring that the reader is compelled to read your book and stays immersed in it. In this set of editing passes, you'll make sure they don't feel confused, irritated, or left out. These friction points add up, and though the reader may not realize why, it bothers them. They may not know why they set the book aside and say, "It was okay. Just not for me." Could be a lot of reasons, but sometimes it's because an otherwise good book has too much friction.

You are in a battle with the world for your reader's attention, and you must fight to keep it if you are going to deliver on your Promise to them. The only time we want a reader to be interrupted and leave the page is when we ask them to stop reading and do something.

Pass #11. Clarity and Assumptions

You've probably read a book that was "hard to get through" or had sections you "had to read a few times." That's frustrating, right? You know there's some good content in there, if you could only find it. You know the process the author shares would help you, if you could only follow it.

Because we know our content inside and out, sometimes we don't realize that the way we lay out teaching points and describe processes is not as clear as it could be. We also make assumptions about what our reader already knows and can easily understand. When a reader has to struggle through your content, you can lose them. So for this pass, go to the following content in your book and make sure a person who does not have your experience or depth of knowledge can pick up what you're putting down.

- **Brand-new concepts.** Did you introduce something that you're pretty sure no one has ever thought about? Consider this: It probably took you more than a hot minute to come up with it, so give your reader what they need to come around to your way of thinking. Should you explain how you came up with it? Probably. Would it help to share a counterpoint for comparison? Yup.

- **Research.** Did you include references to research that the reader needs to understand so they can move forward? Make sure you've explained those studies and how they are relevant to specific teaching points, as well as how the research is relevant to the reader. Break it down for them. Simplify it. Give examples, if needed. Also, sometimes we pull quotes from studies and forget to share our take on those quotes. Why did you choose *that* quote from *that* study? It's not always obvious. Tell the reader.

- **Processes and systems.** Did you lay out sequenced information, such as a step-by-step or multilayered process? If so, read through it and make sure your reader can follow it. Did you leave out something crucial, something you thought "everyone would know to do"? You may need examples at each stage to help people catch on.

- **Exercises and action steps.** Did you ask your reader to do things so they could make progress? Building on the Doability pass (#4) above, make sure your instructions are clear.

- **Story references.** Did you reference a person or story more than once in your book? Don't assume your reader will remember the people you've talked about and the stories you've shared. For example, do you remember Sam from Chapter 4? Don't look. Just see if you can conjure up his story in your mind. I'll bet you can't. Frustrating, right? Makes you want to go back to Chapter 4 and find the story, because anytime I ask you to remember something, you figure it's important that you do that. Now I'm taking you out of *this* chapter, which means I am distracting you from the information you need in this moment. The fix is to give more information about Sam so you can easily remember his story or you know enough about him to understand the reference. So, for example, I could edit that text like this: "Remember Sam, the memoirist who lost his husband and got stuck because he felt he hadn't delivered on the promise in his own life, so he couldn't promise it to readers?" Ring a bell, now? Go find your follow-up references to people and stories, and make sure the reader has enough to go on.

- **Terms.** Did you include lingo or industry terms? Make sure you explain them the first time you use them in the body text, even if you also have a glossary of terms elsewhere. Remember, you are going for an immersive experience—you're writing a page-turner. Just as your reader may feel they have to flip back in the book to find a story you've referenced, they will also feel compelled to look up terms they don't understand. I don't know about you, but if I have to go online to figure out what an author is talking about, I'm going to end up checking my email and social media accounts. Now I've set the book down. Who knows when I'll pick it back up again?

- **Pop culture references.** Do you mention songs, movies, TV shows, artists, or celebrities in your book? You don't want your reader to feel left out. Don't assume everyone will understand your pop culture references. If you want to mention a movie or song, give context. Even if you think, as I do, that every human knows the song "Purple Rain" by Prince, I'm still going to explain that it's the greatest rock ballad of all time. (Fight me.) And if I were to talk about the song within a story, I would also describe what the song sounds like. I might mention the melancholy guitar riff and how the song builds and builds until it feels like a religious experience, like listening to gospel. I'm getting chills right now just thinking about the melodic guitar solo. I might also mention that it's kinda awkward to roller-skate to it, but man, I sure did try—every Saturday from age eleven to thirteen.

- **Quotes.** Did you include quotes you love in the body text? While you don't have to explain why you included quotes below the chapter or section headers (epigraphs), if you include them in the body text, make sure you explain to the reader why that quote is relevant. When you just plop a quote into the middle of a paragraph or even between paragraphs, it interrupts the flow. If you do it more than once, this can be jarring for readers.

Once again, these are surgical edits. Little inserts here and there that make a world of difference to the reader, and they'll never even notice it. That's the point, remember? It's when they *do* notice that you have a problem. You want their reading experience to be as seamless and immersive as possible.

Pass #12. Redundancies and Unintentional Repetitiveness

I can say with 100 percent confidence that you wrote some of the same stuff more than once. That's normal in a first draft. You're sorting out your ideas and trying to find the best way to say this or that. So don't be alarmed when you go through this pass and find a bunch of redundancies.

Now let's talk about repetitiveness, which is overused words and phrases. To be clear, repetition is totally okay if you do it with intention. Writing lyrical prose, for example, or for emphasis. Most of the time, though, we repeat words unconsciously. When a reader starts to notice, we've probably used that word at least five times in quick succession. As we've established, you don't want your reader to notice this stuff.

You can locate some of your repeats using the Find function in Word. Start by looking for the words that you know you've used a lot. If you're writing a business book, start with the word "business." When my authors work on this in workshop, they often try to come up with synonyms for the words. A more effective fix is to try and rework the sentence to eliminate the repeated word.

Editors will catch a bunch of them for you. Still, try to find and fix as many as you can on your own.

Pass #13. Accessibility and Learning Styles

IKEA furniture and I are not friends. One hot summer night, I found four large boxes on our front porch. Four boxes that were supposed to be our new couch. With my wife at work and our ten-year-old at a sleepover, I was on my own. I won't get into the details; just know that four hours later, I was on my living room floor surrounded by cushions and boards and screws and other thingies, sweating profusely from the heat, looking up liquor delivery on my phone. I rarely drink, so that should be all you need to know about how the night went. Oh, and I was pantsless. (Again, it was really effing hot.)

IKEA and I are not friends because, like many people, I'm not so great at figuring things out from just a picture. Some of your readers may be able to grok a new concept the first time they read it. Others may need a story, or for you to walk them through a potential scenario to help them understand it. And some may need all that, *plus* a diagram or contextual model. Be mindful of the fact that we all have different learning styles. Try to make your content as accessible to as many people as possible by providing layers of explanation. You won't need to do this for simple teaching points, but it will really help your reader if you provide narrative and/or visual examples to help them process complicated or challenging teaching points.

For example, in *The Hollywood Approach: Script Your Life Like a Hit Movie and Live Your Wildest Dream*, Kristina Paider uses examples of characters from famous movies to illustrate how readers can overcome obstacles. She doesn't use just one—she uses at least three, and they are the *same* three characters throughout the book, so readers can easily build off the previous examples. This makes her content, which is advanced screenwriter stuff applied to personal growth, super easy to follow for everyday folks. Genius.

Pass #14. Feedback Protocol

The only way to know if your book works for your Ideal Reader is to ask them to read it and give you feedback. A crucial step in the editing process involves sending your manuscript to people who actually need it along with a set of questions designed to give you the insights you need to figure out if your book really works. After you receive their responses, you'll look for patterns and edit accordingly. In Chapter 14, you'll learn the Feedback Protocol I use with all the books I write and teach my authors in Top Three Book Workshop.

Pass #15. Sources and Citations

I hate creating citations. Like, a lot. Especially for articles found on the web. Author, title, website, date issued, date accessed. (Good luck remembering that last one.) When I'm writing, I usually copy and paste links to articles into a comment or footnote and leave it there until the very last second I have to deal with it. It's my passive-aggressive attempt to get my editor to take pity on me and do it for me. They never do. They'll fix my screwed-up sourcing, but that's about it.

Hopefully you've also left yourself breadcrumbs so you can easily create citations where needed. You'll have to cite data and other research, quotes from articles, and even ideas from other authors.

If you're quoting a line or two from a book, you can easily weave it into the body text like this:

In her must-read book for almost-entrepreneurs, *Dream Bold, Start Smart*, visionary accountant Tatiana Tsoir explains what readers can expect: "By the end of this book you will know exactly how to do what you love and avoid costly mistakes, and you will be empowered to build something special for *yourself*."[6]

For article references and research, I recommend you create proper citations (yuck!) in the footnotes (at the bottom of the page) or endnotes (at the end of the book). Either option is fine. If you're trying to decide, ask yourself if your reader would prefer footnotes or endnotes.

Since your editor probably won't take pity on you either, refer to *The Chicago Manual of Style* to create your citations in accordance with their guidelines. This is the standard style guide for books published in the US.

Pass #16. Submission Checklist

Many new authors make common mistakes. Heck, I've written dozens of books and I still make plenty of them. After a super-word-geek email exchange with a few copy editor friends, I asked them to help me create a Submission Checklist. What did they wish authors would fix on their own? It's not comprehensive by any means, but it sure covers a lot. This is your last pass before submitting to your editor, and you may find it frustrating at first because you probably weren't aware of your

---

6   Notice that Tatiana included the Promise she created in Top Three Book Workshop in her book, word-for-word. Yes, I pulled this quote from her book on purpose.

writing tics. Once you get through it, though, your manuscript will be much cleaner and tighter, and your editor will be thrilled because they'll be able to focus on everything else that needs to be fixed. Also, some copy editors won't correct certain issues for you, especially if the problem is pervasive. They'll ask you to fix it, so why not just get it done now and make it easier for them to do a good job for you?

If you'd like to download your own copy of our Submission Checklist, go to the Must-Read website (writeamustread.com/tools).

Life Keeps Happening and So Will Your Book

As I write this, I have affixed to my head about a dozen electrodes covered by two white medical socks. Across my shoulder I sport a black vinyl strap to carry around a small rectangular purse full of wires and whatever device NYU is using to track my brain waves. I'm having an ambulatory EEG, which basically means I am taking an at-home test to see what's up, up there.

When the nurse started the process of pasting wires on my skin, she asked, "Do you have a hair tie?" She said it all casual-like, as though it wouldn't be a big deal if I didn't have one.

I did not have a hair tie.

And I guess it wouldn't be a big deal, unless I want to leave my house. Which I cannot do without kicking off the neighborhood gossip train, like that one time I loaded about twenty boxes into a van to take to the Javits Center in Manhattan for BookExpo, and our neighbor across the street told another neighbor she thought my wife and I were getting divorced.

As it turns out, a hair tie is kind of a big deal when you have a weekend of wearing two socks on your head with a partial ponytail somewhere back there. The rest of my hair is a hot mess of frizzy wisps poking out. If you saw me at Walgreens, you'd ask me if I need you to call someone. Last night we ordered pizza, and my wife wouldn't let me answer the door. Yes, it's that bad.

The thing is, I don't even care. It's just another day in 2021 that didn't turn out as I'd hoped or planned. As I sit here, I also have to keep my right leg elevated due to a dog bite wound that landed me in the hospital for four days with a life-threatening infection. This was just one week after my wife, a COVID-19 long-hauler, had been in the hospital, her third trip since she contracted the virus. No joke. She was in room 238 and I ended up in room 239 exactly seven days later. The nurses looked at me funny, as if to say, "Don't I know you?" Yep. You sure do.

A few days after I was released, I had the worst pain I'd experienced since childbirth, as the IV antibiotics aggravated my spinal stenosis (or so says my doctor) and herniated disc.

So today, I'm sitting here looking sexy with my brain socks, puncture wound, and back pain. If I told you it's also my time of the month, you'd tell me to stop exaggerating.

Why am I spewing this laundry list of issues like my hypochondriac Grandma Peg, who always wore a blazer and fresh lipstick and never stopped talking about her ailments? Because I learned something major in 2021 that up until then I hadn't fully understood. Life happens, and when it *keeps* happening, it's okay to take longer than you planned to finish the thing. It's okay if it's a whole year longer than you'd planned. Or maybe close to two years. It's okay *however long it takes*.

I tell my students in Top Three Book Workshop that it's okay to take the time they need to think, to deal with a crisis, to refocus their concept, even to ditch the book they think they should write for the one that's in their heart. I tell them it's okay to explore, and play, and revel in the delicious unfolding that is the creative process. I tell them breaks are important, their health is important.

For me, though, it was never okay. Especially when it came to finishing my book.

Don't get me wrong. I have missed most deadlines in my life, largely due to my inability to say no to people who need help, and partly due to my delusion that I can write and edit like the wind. But when I had to push back my own book—a book that, after seventeen years of working on other authors' books, will finally have my own name on the cover—it did not feel okay.

I should tell you why I'm wearing this contraption on my head. Until now, I haven't told many people this story, or the whole story, because I'm a very private person. Now I know this story can be of service, so I'm fine sharing it.

On Valentine's Day of 2021, I was writing like mad to meet my book deadline. I stopped to meditate for ten minutes or so and when I went back to my computer and called up an article I needed for research, I couldn't make sense of it. It was as if the words had shifted order on each line, as though chunks of words had moved around to form entirely new, nonsensical sentences.

Almost immediately, my pulse quickened and fear took over.

Why can't I read?

Why can't I read?

Panicked, I tried to read the words aloud, but it came out sounding so strange.

As I walked down the stairs to find my wife, I called down to her on the living room couch. "Something wrong. Can't read."

Within a few minutes, she had me in the car en route to the nearest hospital, which is only three blocks from our house. I had trouble talking. I couldn't find the words I wanted. My arm is tingly, I tried to say, but it came out, "Arm. Problem."

In the ER, a team of people rallied around me. They asked me so many questions. I tried my best to answer, tried to find the right words.

In my mind, a different panic took over. *I'm a word person. I make my living from my brain. What if I can't support my family? What if I can't get the words back? What if they're gone forever?*

Within about half an hour, I started to find my words again, though I was afraid to try to read anything. After another half-hour, I found the same article I had been reading when this started. When I found it, I scrolled to the exact sentence that had confounded me.

I could read it. From start to finish, it made sense.

I read it four more times to just to be sure. I read the signs in my hospital room. I read the captions on the TV. Slowly, I began to calm down. Maybe it was just a fluke. Maybe stress.

"We can't be sure you had one, but I think you had a TIA, which is also called a mini-stroke," the doctor told me. He explained some of my other symptoms, including the numbness in my arm and a slight droop on the right side of my face, which I didn't even notice.

A TIA, or transient ischemic attack, is a temporary blockage of blood flow to the brain. After admitting me to the hospital, they ran a ton of tests on me and found no cause. That led to many more doctor appointments and their tests: cardiologist (heart is A-okay), hematologist (nothing to see here), and neurologist (unremarkable).

This at-home EEG is likely the last one.

Who knows why I lost my words that day? Maybe a test will reveal something in time. Maybe it was stress. My wife nearly died from COVID in 2020, and I had been holding up my family for most of that year. We kept getting hit after hit, and my book deadline kept getting pushed back and back. Each time a health or mental health crisis came up and I realized I couldn't do my work for students and for Mike *and* complete my own book, I had to push the book back. And back. And back. I've lost count of how many times I've had to email my publisher and say, "I can't make the deadline."

None of that felt okay. I teach people how to write books, and I couldn't manage to get my own done. *Not okay.* So not okay, I ended up with a TIA. Or whatever it was.

But pushing my book deadline back again had to be okay. Because *I* had to be okay.

Sometimes life happens and keeps happening and you start to feel as though you'll never finish your book. That was me. And the thing is, as long as your book keeps happening, all that *is* okay.

I kept my book alive in the Notes app on my phone, jotting down ideas while waiting for blood draws. I kept my book alive in writing sprints, sometimes just a few words at a time. I kept my book alive while I worked to keep myself alive, and my family alive, and eventually it got done. Does it really matter that I'm two years behind schedule? Nope. What matters is, I didn't give up. I didn't accept the sequence of unfortunate events as a "sign from the universe" that I shouldn't bother writing my own book. I didn't accept that I'd missed some "perfect" artificial window to release it. And I didn't even accept my own complaints and bad moods about it. I complained to my nearest and dearest and then picked a new deadline.

Onward, onward, ever onward. Tomorrow I get this damn thing off my head, a few steroid shots in my back, and I'll be good to go.

Tomorrow I'll hit "attach" and then "submit." Tomorrow, life will happen—and so will this book.

Your Book in the Wild

The day I finally submitted my revised manuscript for this book to my editor for the last read-through before copy edit, I posted the section you just read as an article on Medium and then shared the link on social media and sent it to my email list. More than any other "Book in the Wild" work I'd done up until then, it was the most impactful. This is because it's a healing story, and I wrote it for my reader. For *you*. Yes, readers want to learn from you, but what they really want from you is to be inspired to carry on and try again.

Once you've completed your editing passes, post an excerpt from your book. Choose one that isn't about tips or frameworks. Go with one of your healing stories. (If you have a traditional publishing deal, you will need permission from your publisher.) Share your excerpt widely. Show your readers the fruits of your labor. Show them how much you care about them. Show them your heart.

P.S. My ambulatory EEG turned out just fine. Onward!

CLAIM YOUR REWARD

Once you've completed your editing passes, go to the Must-Read website (writeamustread.com/rewards) to unlock a special gift from me.

Edit for Revenue and Reader Engagement

YOU HAVE BIG PLANS. The fact that you're reading this book tells me that you want to help people, you really do. You also hope that, in doing so, you can move further down the path toward your own dreams. Maybe you hope to increase your client list, or expand your network, or launch a public speaking career. Perhaps you are on the visionary path. Whatever it is, you've got to consider it now, during the writing process, so that you can get ready for it.

Inexperienced authors tend to think about their book plan in stages. First I'll publish the book. Then I'll worry about everything else. The problem with that way of thinking is, you may end up missing out on the opportunities.

After all your hard work writing a transformational, must-read book, I'm sure you want to reap the rewards of engaging with your readership. Beyond just feeling awesome when they tell you how much your book helped them, you can build your email list and social media following; sell programs, products, and services; drive people to your website; and inspire people to spread the word about your book. That's the good news. The other news, which isn't bad, per se, but may make you want to scream, "AJ, I've done everything you asked. I have nothing left!" is you have to figure this out *before* you finish editing your manuscript. Why? Because if you don't know how you want to engage with readers, you'll likely leave it out of your book and miss countless opportunities. You may feel overwhelmed just thinking about all the options, but man oh man, don't drop the ball on this one.

In this chapter, we'll talk about #17 on the Must-Read Editing Pass Checklist, the editing pass that ensures you are ready for reader engagement.

How Do You Want to Engage with Readers?

Reader engagement is a critical component of authorship, especially if you want to become a career author. And yet, most of the authors I've known never even consider it, much less come up with a plan for it. Fewer still take action on that plan. I'm not sure why. Perhaps they haven't caught up to the digital/social media age and still imagine that red rope between authors and their readers. Maybe it's imposter syndrome rearing its ugly head again, post-release, telling them that their book sucked, so why bother? Or maybe they see their pub date as the finish line, not realizing that it's really the starting pistol for a very long race.

Modern publishing makes it nearly impossible to write from your cave and only come out for book tours. Even J.D. Salinger, the author of *The Catcher in the Rye*, couldn't be J.D. Salinger the recluse today. Readers expect to have at least some sort of access to you. And anyway, since your aim is to write a must-read book that truly changes lives, wouldn't you want to hear about the transformation your book inspires? I'm sure you do want to know about it. But how? Do you want your readers to email you? Find you on social media? And which platform? Do you want your readers to listen to your podcast? Seek you out at conferences? Join your email list? Follow and read your blog?

When I bring this topic up with my authors, it is typically in the context of one of the book launch and marketing classes I teach in workshop. I introduce it early in the course because I want them to start setting up their author platform and begin talking about their book as soon as they land on their Ideal Reader. (I asked you to talk about it right away, too. I hope you did!) An author platform is your reach, your sphere of influence. Simply put, it's your ability to sell books. This is a book about writing, not marketing, so I won't go into it much deeper here.

You don't have to do all the things, but if you want your book to live past publication date and grow a loyal readership, please don't submit your manuscript for edit before you've at least given some thought to how you want to show up for your readers, and how you want them to show up for you.

Here is a simple framework to organize your thoughts.

What does your reader want? Consider how your Ideal Reader may want to connect with you. Are they the type who want to continue learning with you, and in person? Would they like to read new stuff from you from time to time? Do they want to see more about how you live your life? Will they need or want more inspiration from you on a regular basis? Where do they hang out offline and online? Prioritize your reader's habits and interests, not what other authors do. You may get inspiration from other authors, but that doesn't mean you have to do what they do, nor should you. Reader First!

What do you want? Once you have a list of ideas about how to connect with your reader after publication, think about what *you'd* like to do. Do you love meeting people one-on-one or in groups? Or not at all? Do you prefer recording videos over writing newsletters, articles, or blogs? Can you keep up with social media, or do you hate it with the fire of a thousand suns? How much of your life do you feel comfortable sharing with the public?

When you set the terms for connection, most readers will happily follow your lead. I've mentioned my friend Julian Winters, author of young adult fiction. He is a master of showing up for his readers while protecting his time and privacy. He posts regularly on the two plat-forms his readers use the most, sharing a lot of pictures about the life of a writer. He also posts about things he loves—books, comic books, movies and TV shows, music, and food. His readers feel like they know him, but if you look closely at his feeds, you'll see that he doesn't share much about his personal life. Hardly anything, in fact. That's on purpose, and it's worked for him.

If you really don't want to deal with social media at all, you can hire a part-time assistant to help you out. Interns, virtual assistants— even a teenager could do it for you as long as you give them a set of rules to follow. One of my authors had a serious fear of social media because she is a public figure who talks about racial equity and had been harassed online to the point where she had to shut down her social media accounts. I suggested that she hire someone to post and handle comments for her, and alert her to positive comments to which she may want to respond. That way, she can manage the conversation on her book and be somewhat accessible to readers while protecting her safety and mental health.

What is sustainable? Now that you've sorted out what your reader wants and what you want, the final consideration is sustainability. I'm always surprised when authors tell me they've never thought about this, because as I said in the introduction, a book is forever. Do you want readers to try to book appointments with you five years from now? Do you still want to host events ten years from now? Now, "forever" is not really forever in this context. Most people understand that a twenty-year-old book may have some obsolete references. Still, your book can help you grow your business or brand long after publication if you are simply thoughtful about what's doable long term. Sure, it's easy enough to post a message that says you're no longer doing this or that, but wouldn't it be better if you could drive people where you want them to go even ten years out? So think about what you can actually keep up for the next ten or so years.

If you don't want to connect with readers at all, I implore you to at least set up an email list and send something to that list once a month. It could be a short piece of writing, or a recipe, or a favorite picture from your phone. You could crowdsource content from your readers by asking them to share their experiences after your book and choose the best to share in your newsletter. You don't have to put out personal details or communicate frequently. Just do something and do it consistently. Your readers are worth it, and so is your book—and the next book you write that you want to promote to your readership!

How Do You Want to Make Money from Your Book?

Putting your reader first does not mean you ignore your own needs or goals. The beauty of writing a reader-focused book that truly delivers is that your life absolutely will change. You will have more opportunities. Some doors that were previously closed will open for you. What do you want those opportunities to be? What changes do you want to see? You can wing it and see what comes up. Or you can set your intention and direct the reader toward the offers you want them to take and toward the stuff and experiences you want to create or expand.

Perhaps your plan is simply to become an author and you don't want to generate income outside of book sales. I totally get that, in which case you can skip this section. (And yes, as I shared in Chapter 1, you *can* make money from book sales.) But most of my authors do want their book to change some aspect of their lives. They want to start or grow a business around their Core Message. They want to serve their Ideal Reader by providing additional services and/or products. They want to become a speaker or book more gigs, or better gigs, or both. They want to become a thought leader. A personal brand. A noted authority. Perhaps all three. Sometimes they have all that but they want more of it, or want to reshape it into something more powerful and authentic. Some want more followers, listeners, clients, or business connections. Some of my authors want movie deals.

Whatever it is you want, you are more apt to get it if you plan for it and plant seeds for that plan in your book. I'll get into that next. For now, brainstorm *how* you plan to get what you want. Will you hold retreats? Workshops? Trainings? Conferences? Summits? Do you want to work with people one-on-one? Are you hoping to launch or up-level your speaking career? Do you want more podcast listeners? Do you have an evergreen program you want readers to buy?

You don't need a grab bag of offers, and your offers may have a shelf life. Again, this is about what your readers need and want, and what *you* need and want. Once you have a list, pare it down to what is most important and sustainable.

One last note about monetizing your book: Yes, it's okay to use your book to get what you want. It's okay to want something more or something new. And it's okay to want big things. We've never met, but I know you well enough to be sure that you have good intentions. I know this because you're still here, reading this book. I mean, we're just about at the end, and I've asked a lot of you. I've asked you to face fears and set your own needs and ego aside to support your reader. I've asked you to push yourself to give your reader everything they need, to create something truly remarkable for them, to write a book that becomes a must-read. And you didn't bail. You've stuck with it, even when you may have wanted to give up. You really do want to make a difference, of that I'm sure. So go get your life.

Plant Seeds in Your Manuscript

Once you've figured out how and when you want to engage with readers and how you want to earn additional revenue from your book, plant some seeds to ensure those intentions grow.

To be clear, I'm not talking about a pitch. Avoid the salesy stuff at all costs; it really turns readers off. I'm not talking about teasing the reader with *some* of what they need and then asking them to buy the remaining 20 percent. And I'm not talking about littering your book with testimonials. Planting seeds is about showing your reader how you want them to connect with you by including anecdotes, references, and stories that demonstrate how you interact *now*, even if it's only on a small scale.

Let's say you really want to shift from doing breakout speeches to keynotes, and you hope this book you're writing will help you do that. (It will.) Plant a seed or two about keynotes by referencing an experience you had during one of your speeches, or before or after the speech. It's okay if you haven't done a keynote yet; talk about a different type of speech, and then plant a seed about the keynote by referencing how you crafted the speech or what inspired it.

What if you want people to follow your blog or subscribe to your podcast or YouTube channel? You could include a reference to it in your bio, sure. You could include an ad at the end of your book. But if you really want people to start consuming additional content from you, plant the seed. Talk about a listener who blew your mind with a comment you didn't expect. Share how you plan your content. Reference an interview you did that cemented a belief or changed your mind about something.

You want more clients? Share content about clients and about how you worked with them. This is not a testimonial; this is you sharing an anecdote that includes you. A key distinction.

Want to do workshops, events, or trainings? Share something about how you created the event, or why. Include attendee/student experiences to illustrate teaching points and help get in front of reader doubts and criticisms. For examples of this approach, read this whole damn book.

Do you see how it works? Planting seeds for revenue and reader engagement is not about overt promotion. It's about showing your reader how they could experience you outside of the book.

Before we move on, an important caveat: The seeds you plant must be in service to the reader. A shocker, I know. This strategy is not about manipulation or pressure. It's about finding anecdotes, references, and stories that will help your reader, or help you connect to your reader, and then framing that content in a way that plants seeds for the change you want to see in your life. When you reread sections of this book, notice that references to the work I do with authors is in service to *you*. I've included examples and explanations that help you better understand my teaching points, help you move past insecurities and keep going, help you shift your mindset in important ways. At this point, I do this automatically. I didn't have to think about the stories or anecdotes that would show you I love my workshop and want to keep doing that. I already had them in my Content Inventory.

However, I did have to think up an offer that would be more accessible to readers than my workshop. This anecdote is actually a great example of figuring out how to offer the reader a way to engage in a way that suits your needs. I didn't want you to be priced out of the experience of continuing to learn from me and I needed a scalable offer, so I created Top Three Authors' Club, the weekday writing sprint group I mentioned in Chapter 8. I figured I could make that affordable for you and easily serve a lot of people. I knew it had value because it helped my workshop authors stay the course and finish their books. And I knew people wanted it, because I had a list of people waiting for me to launch something for folks who didn't want to or couldn't take the workshop.

Now, you absolutely *can* give readers a way to access your offers. I like to mix it up. I might include a URL for free resources in the body text and then include a different URL for an offer in a footnote or call-out box.

You can also include one heartfelt, transparent ask. No gimmicks. Just a sincere request to do this or that. You'll have to earn it first, of course. Maybe you want to include an author's note at the back of your book. Feel free to do it, as long as it's genuine. Once you've earned a reader's trust and delivered on your Promise to them, they will be more than happy to consider your request.

Your Book in the Wild

If you aren't sure what you want to offer readers, ask them directly. Come up with a few ideas and post a poll on your social media and/or send it to your list. Or ask an open question about what they'd like to hear more about from you. Remember to mention your book and to share your Reader Statement, Core Message, and Promise when you pose the question. You want to hear from Ideal Readers, not just anyone with an opinion.

You can also try this to figure out how your readers may want to engage with you.

Onward!

Make Sure Your Book Actually Works

"**I**'M READING YOUR book and I feel like it was meant for me."

This was one of the responses Linda Ugelow received when she sent her manuscript for her book, *Delight in the Limelight*, out for reader feedback. When she shared this comment on her social media, I did one of those cheesy air fist pumps. Good thing my teenager didn't see me.

I'm reading your book and I feel like it was meant for me.

Yup. That's the goal. That's the ultimate prize. When your Ideal Reader feels that way about your book, you know your book works. You know you did your job as an author and really, truly pulled it off.

Linda had been working on *Delight in the Limelight* for years, the last two and change in Top Three Book Workshop. She worked on it steadily and at her own pace. In Chapter 5, I shared a bit about how she took breaks from time to time to test drive her content through in-person and online workshops and through speeches. Linda made writing sprints a part of her daily schedule; she is one of the few people who keeps her camera on during dance breaks. In her approach to writing and editing her manuscript, she was thoughtful, curious, and so very dedicated to serving her Ideal Reader. Linda had a goal—she wanted real transformation for her readers, and she was willing to put in the work to achieve it.

Following the Feedback Protocol I teach in workshop, and which you'll learn in just a hot second or so, Linda sent her manuscript to Ideal Readers after she completed all the passes in the Must-Read Editing Method and a round of developmental/substantive edits with me.

In addition to the "your book was meant for me" comment, she also received these gems:

"This book is true thought leadership. I've read dozens, maybe hundreds of books on public speaking; taken courses/classes/rehearsals, etc. I've given dozens of talks. I have NEVER seen anything like this. Thank you!!!!"

"Reading this book made me excited to do the work, eager to transform and step into my own personal limelight."

"I would love to bring this book to my book club."

So let's pause for a moment. Let's review the Reader Transformation Sequence I first shared in Chapter 1:

Buy. Readers will buy your book because you have a solution for their problem.

Read. Readers will read your book because you see them and you get them.

Finish. Readers will finish your book because they trust you.

Act on. Readers will follow the advice in your book because you believe in them.

Tell. Readers will tell people about your book because *they* believe in *you*.

By staying true to Reader First through the development of her Core Message and Promise all the way through her editing passes, Linda wrote a book that satisfied all five steps. (Okay, they didn't have to buy it, but I think in this case, that one is a gimme.) How did she know her hard work had been worth it? She had proof from readers. And not just any readers—her Ideal Readers.

In her post sharing the comments, Linda wrote, "I've been over-come with emotion this week after receiving the first advance reader responses for *Delight in the Limelight*. After four years of learning to write a book that will transform a life, it feels like a mission accomplished."

Mission accomplished indeed, Linda.

Feedback from Ideal Readers is a critical self-editing pass that you need to take before you move on to production, which begins with your copy edit. If your book doesn't work, what's the point? You have to find out if your ideas make sense, your processes produce results, and your stories are helpful. You have to find out if the book does what you set out to do. And getting feedback doesn't mean asking people to tell you what they think. You need specific answers to specific questions.

Ideal Readers Only!

We all want approval from people in our field—colleagues, experts, and mentors who can give us their "professional opinion" about the quality of our books. And we would love it if our family and friends would tell us all the stuff we need to hear, about how awesome we are and how proud they are of us. The thing is, your mom isn't going to tell you the truth about your book. Well, my mom probably would, but that's because she's an editor. She'd be nice about it, but she'd tell me. Most moms would not. Your best friend, your spouse, your colleague down the hall—they care more about their relationship with you than they do about your reader, and that will lead them to withhold the truth.

We also yearn for feedback from a mentor or expert who can vali-date our theories and make us feel better about our research or ideas. Yeah, there's merit to that, for sure. And, depending on your topic, you may need someone to sign off on it. Approval of any kind is great, espe-cially when we are putting ourselves out there in such a vulnerable way.

That said, the most important advance reader is someone who has a lot in common with your Ideal Reader, someone who is living with a similar set of circumstances and wants the same things. And it's crucial that your advance reader is *not* someone you know well, who will likely feel pressure to say nice, encouraging things to you.

How do you find your readers? You can start making a list of prospects the second you have a Reader Statement. If you forget to do that or haven't yet come up with enough people, you can post the statement on social media or ask around. You don't have to say yes to everyone who offers. Be discerning. Even when you ask people to self-identify using the Reader Statement, sometimes people will volunteer even if they don't fit the bill.

Remember, your advance readers are not the same group as the experts and influencers you want to endorse your book. My workshop authors get this confused from time to time. Your advance readers are the people who need your message and guidance. Remember: a book is not about something, a book is *for* someone. They are your "someone."

WORKSHOP: GET FEEDBACK FROM IDEAL READERS

AFTER MORE than a decade refining the advance reader process, I have this down to a science, and I'm going to give the whole Feedback Protocol to you now. If you want to look behind the scenes at my own advance reader process for this book, go to my website (writeamust read.com/behindthebook).

1. Choose people who are your Ideal Reader. Make sure you get at least ten people to agree to do it, because some won't follow through.

2. Create a list of questions for your readers. We typically have nine questions because ten or more seems daunting. Challenge yourself to ask very specific questions that will help you understand if they "get it." Here are the questions I always ask:

- How would you describe [book title] to a friend?

- Which lessons and ideas stayed with you after you finished reading the book?

- Which stories or anecdotes were the most memorable?

- Which concepts or ideas, if any, seemed confusing?

- How was [book title] useful to you?

- What, if anything, is missing from this book?

- Did the flow of information work for you?

- What type of person would most benefit from this book?

- What do you feel about yourself, your capabilities, and your future after reading this book?

3. Make sure your readers know that your manuscript is an unedited copy and you don't need or want them to correct any typos or errors. You may have edited it, but "unedited" really means a professional copy editor has not gotten their hands on it yet. Few people know the difference between developmental/substantive editors, copy editors, and proofreaders, so don't expect your readers to.

4. Give them two weeks to read the manuscript and send back the answers to your questions. Most will turn in their feedback right at the deadline, no matter how many weeks you give them, so go with two weeks.

5. Make sure you ask them in advance and tell them what you need from them and when they can expect to get your manuscript.

6. When you get the feedback, look for patterns. Do you notice any similar responses? Make note of them. This tells you which content is working especially well and which content may be confusing for your readers.

7. Then make an editing plan. What do you need to address? What do you need to emphasize more?

8. Make sure you thank your readers. You can include them in your acknowledgments and/or send them a free copy of the book when it's out.

You can prep your materials for this exercise in less than half an hour. The whole process, from start to finish, will take you about four weeks: two weeks for reader feedback and two weeks to review it and make any necessary changes.

You'll know you're ready to move forward when you've dealt with all the feedback you want to address in your manuscript.

Let's dig deeper into how to identify patterns in feedback. If one reader says, "I had to go back and read Chapter 4 twice to understand," and another says, "It would be helpful to get more examples for the process in Chapter 4," then you know that you need to address that. The readers may be using different words, but it's really the same issue.

I'll give you an example: When we reviewed Ideal Reader feedback for Mike's book *Clockwork*, I noticed that several readers mentioned acronyms. One said, "I had a hard time keeping track of all the acronyms." Another said, "Too many acronyms!" Another reader said, "The names for the processes were confusing." They all expressed their confusion in different ways, but they were talking about the same issue. So, because we had three mentions about acronyms, we put that issue on the list of things to address in our final substantive edit. We ended up removing half of them and improved the reader experience.

Sometimes you'll identify a pattern that will require you to write new content. Perhaps you need to take more time to explain something. Perhaps you need a story to show how your system works in real life. Maybe you need to add a graphic or diagram. Or you missed something really big. Maybe you need a new chapter or a few new sections to help your reader make the leap you are asking them to make. Allow enough time to consider reader feedback and edit your book accordingly.

Remember that there will always be outliers—people who have a lone-wolf opinion about something. Don't spend too much time worrying about them. You can't please everyone, and really, all art is subjective. You may not think of yourself as an artist, but I hate to break it to you, if you're writing a book, you're an artist. So remember that what works for most people might not work for a couple of people. Don't focus on those couple. Focus on the patterns and use them for information.

Beware of well-meaning English teachers and other word nerds who think they know best when it comes to writing and editing. They may be right or they may be wrong; they may not know that American publishing follows the rules of *The Chicago Manual of Style* and mistakenly fix something that doesn't need to be fixed.

Occasionally, you will get people who give you very detailed advice about changes. Take it with a grain of salt. What you're looking for is feedback about your book, not how someone else might have written it differently. The acclaimed novelist Neil Gaiman once said, "When people tell you something's wrong or doesn't work for them, they are almost always right. When they tell you exactly what they think is wrong and how to fix it, they are almost always wrong."

Bonus: You can ask enthusiastic advance readers to write a review and/or endorse your book. It's easy for them to create a review after answering the nine questions. In fact, they could take their answer for question #1 (How would you describe this book to a friend?) and turn that into a review. Easy-peasy!

(Just before this book went to typeset, I read a book I think you will find very helpful: *Write Useful Books* by Rob Fitzpatrick. I was thrilled to discover the author also believes in writing a book people want to recommend—and I'm proving that he knows how to do that by recommending *his* book to you. I bring it up now because Fitzpatrick has a much more detailed advance reader process that also starts much earlier than mine. Definitely give it a read.)

Feedback Is Information, Not Criticism

I'm sitting on a small stage at the Playwrights' Center in Minneapolis, Minnesota. I'm seventeen years old, and I'm facing an audience of adults. They are actors, playwrights, directors, and discerning theatergoers. Among them are my mentors and a few people who are superstars in the local theater community. All I want in the whole world is to be a playwright of substance.

My new play has just received a cold reading as part of the Playwrights' Center's Monday night reading series. At the time, this slot was only available to core members—playwrights who had earned a level of membership based on career accomplishments. When a slot opened up with only a short time to fill it, my mentor Buffy Sedlachek had advocated for me to have it.

What is a cold reading? It's the first reading in a play's development process. A play is a collaborative process. You can't write a play on your tiny desk in your tiny room—or at Starbucks, the library, or anywhere else—and then expect it to work on stage. You need actors to read it and then get on their feet with it. You need a dramaturg (like an editor for plays) and/or a director to help you workshop it. It is only when you see and hear the play that you realize what works and what doesn't work, and what you need to do to fix the problems. The cold reading is the first step in that development process—and it's the scariest. Actors, who are reading your script for the very first time, perform it for a live audience. Often, that audience is full of judgy theater professionals who can hear all the flaws, all the moments that didn't land, all the structural problems, all the clunky dialogue.

So here I am, having my very first cold reading in front of people I admire, people who I assume are living the life I want to live. And I'm about to get feedback from them. They can say whatever they want—there are no rules. Earlier that year, I saw a playwright storm out of a cold reading after receiving a comment from the audience. I'd heard comments such as "I couldn't relate to the characters at all" and "Do you really need the second act?" For a writer who has lived with their work for months, and sometimes years, comments like that are knife cuts to the soul. What would the audience say to me? Would they take pity on my tender, teenage self, or would they eviscerate me?

Earlier that day, Buffy had taken me aside and shown me how to handle audience notes. She said, "Never, ever argue with feedback. Comments are information. Some of that information will be helpful and some of it won't. It's your job to figure out which comments you want to address and which comments you want to toss out."

That made sense, and I dutifully took notes in my spiral notebook, a leftover from high school.

Then Buffy taught me her secret for handling feedback in the moment—what to do when you're on display, receiving comments from people who are likely waiting for your reaction. She said, "Take that notebook on stage with you. When you hear a comment that may be useful to you, thank the person who gave you the comment, and write it down. When you hear a comment that you know is off the mark, or condescending, or just plain rude, thank the person who gave you the comment, and then in your notebook, write, 'Jerk in the third row needs a hair transplant' or 'F you, lady in red.'"

I was shocked. As my mentor and teacher, Buffy had always been super professional. Now here she was telling me to write "F you" in my notebook.

As the comments rolled in, I jotted down those that gave me helpful information and made naughty comments about the people who offered up snide remarks. As instructed, I smiled and said "thank you" for every comment. I survived that experience, and promptly had a migraine the next day as the pent-up stress left my body.

Over time, I learned not to let my nerves get the best of me. Eventually I stopped having nerves at all. I looked at the audience as a gift—they agreed to listen to my raw work and give me helpful information. Now I have nerves of steel. I read a comment from an editor and I have no emotion. If I have to read the same comment over and over because I haven't nailed my edits, that's super frustrating, for sure. But ultimately, the comments are still information. Because you see, if the audience didn't understand something, that was on me. If they couldn't connect to the characters, that was on me. The same is true with books. If your readers don't understand something, if they can't connect with you, that's on you.

If someone in the audience said, "I don't understand why this character did that thing," my instinct was to explain it, or to respond with, "How can you not see it? It's right there! It's so obvious!" The thing is, it probably wasn't. Maybe that person was an outlier, true. Or maybe other people in the audience agreed with her. I would look around the room for nodding heads, to see if other people felt the same way, or shaking heads if they didn't.

Remember, feedback is just information that will help you figure out how to make your book better. If you stay focused on Reader First, then the information becomes less criticism and more helpful tool to ensure that you have achieved your goal and provided a transformational, immersive reader experience. That you delivered on your Promise. Did they get it or not get it? What helped them the most? What were they confused by? What took longer to understand than you thought it would?

Sometimes you will have a reader who just doesn't get it, even though you've done your best. You can't write a book that's "reader-proof," but you can do your best to ensure that your book works for *most* of your readers.

Feedback Protocol is your book's cold reading. Just as a play doesn't come alive until actors have embodied the roles, your book doesn't come alive until someone who needs it reads it.

Your Editor Is Not Your Boss

When we got substantive edits back on *Fix This Next* from our editor at Penguin Random House, one of his comments shocked me. It read "Less fan service." Less fan service? What the heck? Now, I valued his advice greatly. He worked with us on three books and his insights were invaluable. He pushed us toward clarity, and that's everything. Still, I knew that note was off the mark. "Less fan service" meant he wanted fewer stories, anecdotes, and Mike-isms in the manuscript, the content that is directed at pleasing Mike's readership.

I called Mike and read him the comment.

He said, "Yeah, that's not going to happen."

We both had the same reaction because, first and foremost, Mike puts his readers first. He is writing the book *for* them. He is thinking about his readership, the people who have stayed with him from his first book, the people who love his voice, his point of view, and his heart. And those people, they sure do love a good Mike story. Further, if part of the reason he has fans is because of his stories and his style, why would we have less of that in a book that we know will be a first Mike read for many? His style is a selling point; it's part of the experience, and we've heard from so many readers who love that aspect of his books.

"Fan service" is not a bad thing, as long the content actually does serve them, and as long as it does not leave new fans out. For example, if you were to include an inside joke that only people who have read your other books would get, and then not explain that joke so that new readers can understand it, that would be irritating for new readers. You have to assume that you have new readers with every book. That said, you *can* call back to previous books as long as you explain why you are doing that.

If you are writing your first book, you might be wondering if this applies to you. Yes, it does. Even if you just share posts occasionally on social media, you likely have followers. Isn't your book for them? The people who are already engaged with you? The people who like your style? When they read your book, they want it to be an authentic "you" experience. They want more of you.

In case you're wondering, we got to keep our "fan service."

Your Book in the Wild

Put out a request for Ideal Readers. You may already have a list of people who want to read your book and people *you want* to read your book. Again, you are looking for Ideal Readers. To find them, post this message on social media and/or send it to people who may know someone:

"I'm looking for advance readers for my new book so I can make sure it delivers on its Promise. My book is for _____ who want _____ but are struggling with _____.
Do you know anyone who may be a good fit?"

Onward!

CLAIM YOUR REWARD

Once you've completed your Feedback Protocol, go to the Must-Read website (writeamustread.com/rewards) to unlock deleted content from this chapter and other cool and useful stuff.

Bonus—A No-BS Crash Course in Publishing

THIS BOOK IS not about getting published, but . . .

I hadn't intended to write a chapter on the business of publishing. Then I sent out a pre-questionnaire to my advance readers and nearly all noted they hoped my book would help them figure out how to navigate the publishing world. I sighed dramatically and all but stomped my feet like a child. *But that's not the point of this book!*

Except, hang on, Anjanette.

Your Ideal Readers want it. And a book is not about something. A book is *for* someone. This book is for them and they want to know how publishing works.

And you do teach this topic in your book workshop. You teach it because you want your authors to be informed so they can make better decisions. So they're not taken for a ride. So they know how to vet opportunities.

And you know good and well, Anjanette, that if they don't know what's up, if they remain in the dark about how publishing works and *why* it works that way, they may easily find themselves on a path that will hurt their chances to write and publish a must-read book. Or maybe kill their fire for their book, so they let it sit in boxes in their garage while tumbleweeds roll across their Amazon book listing.

Huh. I guess I better write the chapter.

"I DIDN'T know what I didn't know." This is what I hear from students and other folks who show up to events where I share publishing knowledge. When we don't know what we don't know, we rely on experts, right? We trust them to tell us what we need to know to make decisions, and they will handle the "inside baseball" stuff. That's why they're certified, degreed, and so on. That's why we pay them the big bucks—so we can exhale about all the ins and outs of this and that and get on with our lives.

Here's the problem with that approach in authorship: many so-called experts leave out important information that would help you make a better decision. And by experts I'm referring to some book coaches, book programs, ghostwriters, editors, book launch coordinators, "publishers," and publishers (you'll know the difference by the end of this chapter). I've worked with many authors who, even after they've been published, had very little understanding of the industry. And because they missed out on some basic info, they also missed out on opportunities to get a better deal, to save money, to make more money, to get the word out about their book, and to sell more books.

Some so-called experts are only knowledgeable about one aspect of publishing. You'd be hard-pressed to find a traditional publishing professional who knows enough about self-publishing to guide you. On the flip side, self-publishing "experts" tend to toss out traditional publishing as if choosing that path is ridiculous and no one should consider it—even when they tout their self-published authors who went on to get traditional deals as major success stories for their programs. You can't have it both ways, people! The reality is, self-publishing "experts" don't often know that much about the traditional side of the industry.

I get it—traditional publishers are not in the coaching or educating business. When you sign with them, you are on a need-to-know basis. Self-publishing "experts" either don't know much about the path they diss on or they don't want *you* to know about it because you might question their own methods. For example, a big reason they pooh-pooh traditional publishing is because it takes "so long" to get a book to market. They don't tell you why it takes a long time, and how that benefits you, or what you miss out on because you choose to self-publish. (I will. Don't worry.)

And quite a few so-called experts aren't even experts in *one* thing. Because it's so easy these days, it's common for people to self-publish a book and then decide they are an expert in that area. After just one book, they start teaching classes and coaching. But they don't know much beyond their own experience. Certainly, their experience has value. But at the same time, they don't know what they don't know.

Michael Port once gave me a major compliment that I've never forgotten. In the introduction to this book, I mentioned that I met Michael for the first time when he and Mike Michalowicz asked me to help coach authors at their author retreat in Maryland.

After the first full day, Michael said, "I've known a lot of ghostwriters, but I've never known one who knows the [publishing] business like AJ does."

Mike agreed.

I blushed because I don't take compliments well. At the break, I wrote down Michael's words so I would never forget them. And when I got home from the event, I called my mom to tell her what he said. Why was this compliment so important to me? Because I busted my ass to earn it.

Here's how it started. About three years into my ghostwriting career, I worked with a client who would later become a dear friend. As most of my clients did, Andy came to me through referral. He had a deadline to meet, and his previous ghostwriter had just given him a draft that sounded nothing like him.

When I read the manuscript, it was clear we had to start over, so I advised Andy to ask his publisher for an extension.

"I can do that?" he asked. "Won't they cancel my contract?"

"Not necessarily," I said. "It never hurts to ask, and they want your book to be worth reading, so it's in their best interest to give you the extension. If they agree, get it in writing so you're not in breach of contract."

This conversation sparked other questions throughout the year or so we worked together. Andy would ask me about this or that, and I'd do my best to answer. This was the first time I realized that, through experience, I'd accumulated enough knowledge to be considered an expert in my own right. Except I knew better. I knew that my expertise was limited to my experience.

It was when Andy, a marketing expert, failed to sell many books that I decided I had to learn about the entire industry, not just my corner of it—and that included book marketing. If I really wanted to help Andy and authors like him, I had to educate myself. So I did. That year, I attended my first BookExpo, which, before COVID-19 killed it, was once the largest publishing industry event in North America. My lanyard around my neck, I sat in the back rows of panel discussions I thought my authors might learn from and took copious notes. I walked several football fields of the convention floor, meeting with vendors I thought my authors might benefit from knowing. I loaded up on brochures and other stuff my authors might want.

That began my self-directed education. I soaked up everything I could, attended conferences and book events large and small, and learned the ins and outs of every publishing path: self-publishing, traditional publishing, and hybrid publishing. I'm still doing that, because there's always more to learn.

Since that first BookExpo, I've had many roles in this world: ghostwriter, co-writer, developmental editor, managing editor, substantive editor, acquisitions editor, traditional publisher, project coordinator, book coach, teacher. I'm probably leaving something out. I've written and edited nonfiction for solo authors and for book collections. I've edited novels and short stories—contemporary fiction, mostly, but also literary fiction, and some fantasy and sci-fi. I've made magic for a lot of people and let a few people down because I couldn't finish their projects. I've worked with well-intentioned and flawed people, salt-of-the-earth people, and dishonest people. I've seen crappy books hit the bestseller lists and brilliant books languish in cardboard boxes. I've seen the rise of unknown authors to respectable successes and a precious few to major, world-bending successes. I've seen many more authors' dreams dashed because of this or that reason—often, because they are unwilling to put in the work to get the word out about their books, but just as often because they didn't understand how publishing works. They didn't do the work or they couldn't advocate for themselves because they didn't know what they didn't know.

I loathe laundry lists of accomplishments, so I shared all that begrudgingly. I had to do it, though, because you need a sense of the depth and breadth of my experience so you know who you're dealing with. You can weigh my advice against that experience and then take it all with a grain of salt and do your own homework. Because I don't want you to think I'm *the* go-to expert and then never find out for yourself what would be best for you. I want you to ask questions. I want you to consider your options. I want you to stick up for yourself and ask for more and better, and you can't get more and better if you don't know what to ask in the first place.

Basically, I want you to stop listening to assholes (sorry, Mom) and amateurs, and to do that, you need knowledge.

You're about to get a crash course in publishing, AJ style.

How to Choose a Publishing Path

To get your book to market, you have three primary paths: traditional, self-publishing, and hybrid. I use the word "primary" because you have options on each of these paths. For example, traditional publishing is not just the Big Five; there are thousands of publishers from small boutique presses, mid-tier presses, and yes, the biggies. If you want to self-publish, you could take the DIY approach, or hire a company that offers a package to do it for you (yes, that's still self-publishing), or some combo of both. Hybrid publishers can be as different as apples and oranges when it comes to what they offer authors.

Here's a breakdown of the three primary publishing paths.

1 **Traditional.** A traditional publisher acquires publication rights
to your book, which means they have the exclusive right to publish your book in most or all formats (print, ebook, audiobook)
for a specified period, which could be anywhere from five years to
forever. They also get a whole bunch of other rights, but *not* the
copyright to your work. That's yours. Contracts can differ widely,
so you need an agent and/or an intellectual property attorney to
review yours with you so you understand it.

In exchange for publication rights, traditional publishers agree
to pay you a royalty, which is a percentage of monies earned on
your book. Royalties differ based on the format (again: print, ebook,
audiobook). Sometimes you will also get an "advance" when you
sign your contract, which is an advance on royalties paid in three
or four installments over a period of one to two years. You will have
to earn out this advance before you see another dime from your
publisher. So, if you get a $40,000 advance, you'll get $10,000 at
signing, $10,000 when your book goes into production, $10,000
upon publication, and $10,000 about a year later. When you sell
enough books to cover that $40,000, you'll start to see royalty
checks quarterly or biannually.

Traditional publishers do not charge you for anything. Nothing.
Zip. If any publisher asks you for a dime, they are not a traditional
publisher and may be mispresenting their company.

Most but not all traditional publishers follow a rigorous process designed to ensure they publish the best book possible. (More
about that process below.)

Many traditional publishers have trade distribution. What does
this mean and why does this matter? Trade distributors work to get
your book on the library, bookstore, and big box store shelves, featured in book clubs and subscription boxes, and to public schools,
colleges, and universities. You'll often hear so-called publishers say
they have "global distribution," which only means they are fulfill-
ing demand. If you want a sales team trying to *create* demand with
retailers and bulk book buyers, you need trade distribution. The
Big Five have their own distribution machine. Smaller publishers

have trade distribution contracts with distributors like IPG (Independent Publishers Group).

2 **Self.** The self-publishing path simply means you cover 100 percent of the cost of getting your book to market, from book development to printing. You may opt to manage the entire process and build your own team. Or you may want to hire a company that will help you—in which case you may not earn 100 percent of the net revenue.

Important note: If you don't have a deal with a traditional or a selective hybrid publisher, you are self-publishing your book. I want to make that clear because so many authors *think* they have a publisher when they really hired a company to help them self-publish their book. If you want to go this route, no problem; I simply want you to go into it fully aware. For example, most self-publishing packages do not include developmental or substantive editing (which is generally lumped together as "developmental editing"), and I've yet to come across a company that offers these packages *and* trade distribution. Also, because you may think you have a publisher, you may not think twice about letting them take a cut of your royalties or exclusive rights to this or that. Please read the fine print on any terms, and hire an attorney to review contracts.

3 **Hybrid.** Think of hybrid publishers as a mix of traditional and self-publishing. Here you have the standards and distribution options of traditional, for which you are making a monetary investment. Legit hybrid publishers are selective about the books they acquire. They also pay more in royalties than a traditional publisher.

Your challenge will be vetting hybrid publishers, because anyone can use that term to describe their business. In my experience, most are offering self-publishing packages and *not* giving authors what they need to create and distribute a must-read book—or royalties commensurate with their investment. Independent Book Publishers Association (IBPA) has a list of hybrid publishing standards I recommend you download and keep handy during your vetting process.

When my students and clients ask me how to choose a publishing path, they usually start with, "I know I can't get a deal, so..." It's true that traditional publishers and some hybrid publishers are selective, but that doesn't mean that you should assume your title won't be acquired by one. Please think it through rather than make assumptions about what's possible for you. Sure, you may end up self-publishing anyway, but all sorts of publishers look for all sorts of authors, and I wouldn't write off the other paths before you've considered whether they will meet your needs.

Before you rule traditional out, consider your priorities first.

- **Timing.** Most authors are surprised how long it takes traditional publishers to release a book. And, not understanding why that's the case, they may end up believing "experts" who tell them the extended timeline is "ridiculous" and "unnecessary." (It's not. Read the rest of this chapter to find out why.) Top-tier hybrid publishers follow the same timeline as traditional publishers. This is because they both offer trade distribution. If you just started writing your book and you need it out in the next year, self-publishing is your only option. I really hope you won't rush to publish, but still, if you think you have no other option, you're going to have to go the solo route.

- **Expense.** If you have limited financial resources, your best bet is to try to get a traditional deal. This is the only option that will cost you zero dollars, aside from whatever you decide to spend on your own marketing efforts. Traditional publishing will take longer and is not a sure thing, but the work you do to try to get the deal—the book proposal and building your author platform— is never a wasted effort; it will help you sell more books. Of the other two paths, self-publishing is generally less expensive than hybrid publishing.

- **Revenue.** This is a tricky one, because while with self-publishing you'll earn 100 percent of the net revenue, you may sell more books with a publisher that has trade distribution. If you sell the same number of books, you'll make the least amount in royalties from a traditional publisher, significantly more with a top-tier hybrid publisher, and the most from self-publishing.

- **Control.** Contrary to popular belief, you do not give up total control when you sign with a traditional publisher. In most cases, you have input on and can veto your title and subtitle. Your publisher has final say on cover, but they will ask your opinion. If you really hate the cover, you may have to hire a designer to show them what you want. You will have zero control over your release date, pricing, and how your book is positioned to sales teams. You *should* have final say over editorial disputes, but your publisher can opt not to release your book if they feel it will do them harm. For example, if you launch into a racist rant and they ask you to remove it, they can yank your book and cancel your contract if you refuse to comply. For the most part, though, they will listen to you if you push back about an editorial note. (The Feedback Protocol comes in really handy in these instances.) Ask your attorney to review your contract to ensure your publisher does *not* control any future writing about your idea, frameworks, and so on. If having control is a top priority for you, then go with hybrid or self-publishing.

- **Credibility.** When I first started in publishing in 2005, traditional publishing was the only "credible" path. My ghostwriting clients who chose to self-publish did everything they could to hide that fact. It was still considered a "vanity" option, far from legit, and most authors found it difficult to get books on shelves and media attention. That changed rapidly, especially after some notable big-name authors decided to go that route. Because self-publishing does not hold itself to traditional publishing's standards, and because distribution is typically print-on-demand, it can be difficult to get big media attention. Likewise, some stores, big book clubs, and subscription models prefer not to order self-published books. Further, if you are an academic or a high-profile corporate leader, self-publishing is still a no-no, but some hybrid publishers may be a viable option.

- **Distribution.** As noted above, there's a big difference between "global distribution" and trade distribution. If you want the power of a sales team behind you and no barriers to getting your book on bookstore and library shelves, then you need trade distribution, which means traditional or top-tier hybrid are your two options. (And make sure you confirm that *your* book will have trade distribution; not all books get the same treatment.)

  If you self-publish, you can still get access to wholesale distributors that specialize in serving your market if you apply to be a vendor. And if that doesn't work out, bookstores and libraries can still order your book. This is usually done through Ingram Content Group, one of the largest distributors in the world. They have a self-publishing and a small publisher portal. Note that you can get this service on your own for less than fifty dollars, so don't let anyone dazzle you with their "global distribution" claims. It will take you about thirty minutes to load your files and about three days to three weeks (depending on the retailer) to start seeing your book available for sale.

Now that you have the basics about each publishing path, which one will serve your needs best?

An Overview of the Publishing Process

When I started in this industry, self-publishing had really taken off. Once expensive, print-on-demand publishing and online retailers like Amazon made DIYing it more affordable through platforms like the now defunct CreateSpace and through democratized distribution. This lower cost of entry eventually led more people to self-publish, including notable thought leaders, which also boosted the credibility of self-published titles. That's the cool part. The not-so-cool part is that many people who supported authors who chose this path touted the ability to publish fast and on your own terms, and in doing so, tossed out or ignored many of the quality controls traditional publishers require. This is *not* a good thing.

What follows is an overview of the traditional publishing process. We start with this understanding because if we don't, you won't know which quality control you're tossing out. You may want it. I sincerely hope you'll want it. I mean, you're going to the considerable trouble to write a must-read, a book people will treasure and talk about. Don't you think it deserves all the quality controls?

In Chapter 9, I gave you a quick primer on the editing process. You may want to go back and look at that section again before you read on. Also, the following overview does not include all the internal processes a publisher manages—only those that I don't want you to skip if you choose a different path.

Traditional Publishing Process

1   **Write a book proposal and query letter.** To pitch your book to prospective agents, you'll need a strong proposal that includes an overview of your idea, why readers need it, and why you are the perfect person to write it; a deep dive into your target market (Ideal Reader + stats about that audience); a bio about you tailored to your book; a competitive title analysis; your marketing/launch plan; an outline with chapter descriptions; and one to two sample chapters. The query letter is a very short email that includes one paragraph about your book and your market and one paragraph about you.

    Writing a book proposal is a clarifying process that will help you at every stage of authorship, even if you never land an agent. The work is never wasted. For the best advice on book proposals and query letters, check out Jane Friedman.

2   **Find prospective agents.** The best way to find an agent is to ask other authors who they love to work with, and ask them for an introduction. (Do this *only* after you have a draft proposal and query letter.) If you don't know any other authors, turn to the acknowledgments page in the books you love and look for a shout-out to whoever reps that author. Then do your homework. Is that agent open to submissions? If so, what are their requirements? Be

sure to follow their guidelines *to the letter*. Also note that agents sometimes have short windows when they are open to submissions; one of the best ways to find out about that is by following them on Twitter.

(Some mid-tier and small presses accept unsolicited submissions. They may not even require a full proposal; read their guidelines carefully.)

3   **Pitch proposal to agents.** Following their guidelines, pitch your book to agents. This process can take a few months. Be prepared to get critical feedback from them and to revise your proposal further. You may also get different advice from different agents. Rely on author referrals, the agent's track record, and then finally your gut instincts about working with that person. You want someone who will hustle for your book and advocate for you, so again, do your homework!

4   **Agent pitches proposal to acquisition editors.** Once your proposal has been revised to suit their needs, agents will then pitch your book to editors they know are looking for books like yours. This is also called "going out on sub," as in submission. Be sure to ask for copies of pitches. It's your right to ask for that.

5   **Acquiring editor pitches to publisher.** Some editors have the power to acquire titles without further approval, but many pitch the titles they want to their publisher, along with other editors who are vying for the same slots.

6   **Publisher acquires your book.** When a publisher wants your book, they will make an offer through your agent. If it's accepted, they will follow up with a contract. You'll receive the first installment of your advance shortly thereafter.

7   **Write the rest of your book.** Because you are writing a nonfiction book, you can wait to write the remaining chapters of your book until you have a deal in place. (Fiction and memoir authors must complete their entire manuscript before pitching agents.) Note

that this is when publishers start to position your book for the sales team. Yes, that early.

8   **Developmental/substantive edits.** Your developmental or substantive editor (who may have one of various titles) will set an editorial schedule. They may have structural notes for you right from the start, or they may only give you guidance when they've seen a few chapters. After you complete your first draft, you will typically get two rounds of developmental/substantive edits. Sometimes more work is needed on specific chapters.

9   **Copy edit.** When substantive edits are complete, the next step is copy edit. This is officially the start of production and triggers an advance payment. You will have one to two rounds of copy edits.

10 **Typeset.** During the copy edit process, you will receive interior page design samples for your review and approval. After the copy edit, the designer will typeset your book.

11 **Proofread.** You will receive a typeset proof of your book, usually in PDF format. Some publishers still send "pass pages," short for "first-pass pages," which is basically just a print-out of the proof. (If you don't get a print-out, do it yourself. It's important to review a hard copy.) During this time, a proofreader will also review your proof to catch any remaining errors. You may have one to two rounds of proofreading before your final signoff.

12 **Publish.** At least five months later, probably longer, your publisher will release your book.

You can see why traditional publishing takes a long time. The first few steps—writing and pitching a book proposal to agents—can take months and may not yield the results you want. That said, each step in the rest of the process, from acquisition to book release, is essential to ensure your book is a must-read. If you choose to self-publish or go with a hybrid, please make sure you adhere to steps 8 through 12 in the process.

One more note about why traditional (and some hybrid) publishing can take a long time. Earlier in this chapter, I explained the importance of trade distribution. I've heard some publishing "experts" diss traditional publishing because it "takes too long," as if that's a choice publishers make rather than a necessity that *benefits* authors. You already understand the benefits of the rigorous editing process, which does take several months. What you may not realize is that trade distribution adds even more time to the schedule. This is because bookstores purchase their books months in advance. The book-of-the-month club makes their selections months in advance. And so on. To ensure your book has a chance with these opportunities, the sales team has to pitch your book months in advance, and to do that, they need a galley.

A galley is a bound and typeset copy of your book. It is often an uncorrected proof, created in the final stage of editing: proofreading. Since the sales teams needs the galley months before publication, you can see why trade distribution takes so long. And you can also see why this long publishing runway benefits you.

What You Lose When You Publish Too Fast

Fast is not better. Fast means you cut corners—in development, in writing, in editing, and in production. It also means you cut corners in marketing, which can lead to heartbreak. That old adage, "Just because you can doesn't mean you should," applies here. Just because you *can* publish faster doesn't mean you should. No matter which path you choose—self, hybrid, or traditional—you can follow the steps required to turn out a must-read book.

In the previous section, I explained that trade distribution needs a galley months before publication to pitch to bookstores and other sales opportunities. You also need a galley to submit to trade review journals for critical review. As I shared in Chapter 9, trade reviews help bookstores and librarians make buying decisions and also give your book credibility. To include a pull quote from your review on your cover and/or inside your book, and to be featured in trade journal articles about the upcoming season, you'll have to submit for review at least four to six months in advance of your book release. You may also need a galley to secure endorsements and to pitch media, including podcasts, and you may need it months in advance. If you want your book to be included in a gift guide, you'll need that galley months in advance.

Are you getting the "months in advance" theme here?

When you publish too fast, you miss out on so many opportunities to get the word out about your book. A bonus in taking your time with this is, once you have your galley, you can rest easy about your book and focus on your launch. If you are trying to both finish your book and launch it at the same time, you will absolutely cut corners. You may also make yourself sick, because you sure won't get any sleep. It's all energy drinks and fast food for you as you try to meet impossible deadlines.

Don't do that. Just don't.

What You Lose When You Only Sell Your Book on Amazon

I'm old enough to remember a time when Amazon did not exist. Today, if your book isn't on Amazon, *it* may as well not exist. But this behemoth of a retailer is not the only game in town. The problem is, many of us are so accustomed to using them to buy books, we either forget or don't realize that some people, companies, and organizations don't. And some *can't*. Bookstores (that are not Amazon-owned) cannot afford to buy from Amazon because they need deep discounts to make money—just as Amazon does. Bookstores, big box stores like Target and Costco, and online retailers such as Book Depository or Bookshop buy books from distributors—just as Amazon does. Libraries also buy from these distributors, and from others that specialize in the library market. Some reference librarians have a small Amazon budget for books they can't get through distribution, but many do not.

If you decide to self-publish, make sure your book is available everywhere. This goes for ebooks, too. Yes, Kindle corners the market in the US, but not so in other countries. And buying an American book outside of the US is much easier when it's in digital format. So, why cut yourself off from potential buyers by giving Amazon exclusivity?

Sure, you can make a slightly higher royalty and some other perks, but I've found that access to your books in multiple formats is the key to building readership.

If you opt to choose a hybrid publisher or a company that helps you self-publish, make sure print and ebook versions of your book will be available "everywhere books are sold" and "everywhere books are read."

Market the Hell Out of Your Book

Just as this is not a book about publishing, it is also not a book about marketing. That said, I would be doing you a disservice if I didn't stress the importance of your role in the marketing of your book.

Let's get one thing straight: Marketing your book is *your* responsibility. If you think signing with a traditional publisher means you can sit back and write and they'll take care of finding your readers, someone gave you bad information. What they *will* do is push that trade distribution sales engine behind the scenes so your book is more likely to end up on shelves, but getting readers excited to buy your book is all you. Of course there are exceptions. Publishers will pull out all the stops for some authors. Reality TV stars. Movie stars. Political stars. I'm sure you see the theme by now. If you're already famous, no problem. Your publisher will throw some money at marketing your book. They'll do this because you already have a following. They'll also do this for some successful authors' next books. Not the first one, but those that follow the successful book. Again, publishers will do this because that author already has a following.

That said, some traditional publishers will help you amplify your efforts. In other words, they will help you if you help yourself. So please—help yourself. Help your Ideal Readers find your book.

Let's get another thing straight: You probably don't know enough about marketing to figure out if the hybrid publishing package or self-publishing package book launch add-ons to your contract are worth the money. Again, you don't know what you don't know, so you don't know how to ask the right questions. You put your trust in experts who tell you a press release is going to sell your book (it's not) and offer you a bunch of other stuff you could handle on your own, and you do this because you want a publisher—even if it's one that you paid—to handle your marketing for you.

And one more, very important thing I want you to know: You are going to be too tired to market your book. Just expect that. You're writing a must-read. You're putting in the time and effort to create something truly life-changing for your reader, and that's not a walk in the park. You're also navigating the publishing world, which may as well be Mars and can be frustrating in myriad ways. You've pushed yourself to make something out of nothing, and just when you want to take a hiatus from the world, you have to show up and promote that thing. You will be *tired*.

Before I started teaching my workshop, I took Gloria as a private client and shepherded her through the entire process of writing, editing, and publishing her book. The end result: a gem that served her readers perfectly. It had a gorgeous cover that made you want to pick it up and interior page design that inspired you to keep turning the pages. Gloria did everything right—except she dropped the ball on marketing. I had given her all my timelines, resources, and ideas. I met with her and her team to brainstorm more ideas. She had the knowledge and tools she needed to pull it off. And still, she let that book launch with nothing more than an email to her list.

Gloria was tired—too tired to market her book.

The best thing you can do to ensure you don't bail on your book marketing is to anticipate that you are on your own with this and you will be too exhausted to focus on it when your book is done. The solution? Focus on it *now*. Start planning. Start strategizing. Start talking about it. Start building relationships with people who also serve your readership. Start creating content you may want to use to help spread the word about your book. Start brainstorming bonus offers, media pitches, speech ideas—whatever you think you may want to do to support your book. Just start.

Here's a little surprise you may have already figured out: if you've been following all the "Your Book in the Wild" challenges at the end of each chapter, you have already started marketing your book.

Your Book in the Wild

No matter where you are in the writing, editing, or publishing process, and no matter which publishing path you choose, you are ready to put a book page up on your website. This is important because as you talk about your book, as you take action and share about its development, you will want a way to capture interest from potential readers. I have seen authors who are early in the process share their Reader Statement on social media and get dozens of responses, asking when their book will be available. You need a way to collect those names when they express interest.

What goes on a book page? It can be as simple as the Reader Statement, a picture of you, and a link to sign up for updates about the book and its release. If you want to get fancy, you can add a video about your inspiration for writing the book, but it's not necessary. If you want to reveal your Core Message, you could add it. Or not. The same goes for your Promise. When you have your cover, book summary, trade review pull quotes, endorsements, and retailer buy links, add them. For now, keep it simple.

My students are always surprised when I tell them to create this book page, because they don't think they're ready. They are ready, and so are you. So get that page up this week.

Onward!

CLAIM YOUR REWARD

Writing a book is hard, especially if you're doing this on your own. You deserve a reward as you make progress. When you have your book's release date, go to the Must-Read website (writeamustread .com/rewards) to unlock the ultimate prize. Seriously. Do it.

Onward!

O N MY DESK is a picture of my son, Jack, in a uniform. He's holding a basketball under his arm and smiling extra big. He's ten in the photo, and he absolutely loves the game. The only problem—his love for the game did not match his ability to play it. He's a good all-around athlete, but he didn't really know basketball all that well and he didn't seem to have natural talent for it.

That first season, he spent most of his time on the bench. His coaches were dads who also loved the game. They played the kids who could shoot and block, which meant they didn't play Jack—much. When he did get to play, he passed the ball. All the time. He rarely tried to score, even when he had a clear, easy shot.

Still, Jack showed up to every practice and every game.

The next season, he asked to sign up for basketball again. He showed up for every practice and every game. He spent most of his time on the bench. And when he did get to play, he passed the ball.

The following season was the same. He showed up to every practice and every game. He spent most of the time on the bench. When he did play, he passed the ball. Except one time, he *did* shoot—for the wrong basket. His face was red for hours.

The next season, Jack told us, "I want to sign up for basketball."

Whew. Another season of benching it, but okay.

"As long as you're having fun," I said.

"I am," he said without hesitation. Then he added, "And I want to try out for the other league, too."

He'd been playing in a recreational program open to all children, regardless of ability. The teams were made up of kids from area schools and the community. It was good fun. Nothing serious. The "other league" was next-level basketball. Teams played against other teams in the county, and to play in this league, he'd have to try out.

Oh, boy.

Jack was determined. On the day of tryouts, I noticed that the coach for the elite team wasn't just a dad; he coached varsity basketball for a nearby high school. He knew his stuff.

Coach Tyler explained, "We'll have two rosters. The gold roster will play every game. The white roster will play every other game."

Jack asked me to wait for him in the car, so I watched the tryouts from the parking lot, straining to see him among the flurry of thirteen-year-old boys. *Please let him make the team. Please let him make the team. Please let him make the team.*

When he heard he'd made it onto the white roster, his face fell; some of his best friends were on the gold team. Boys he looked up to; boys he wanted to belong with. Still, he didn't complain.

After the first practice, I approached Coach Tyler. He's a quiet, unassuming guy who wore clothes in muted colors like beige and moss green. I asked him why he had added Jack to the team. He said, "That kid has heart, and that can take you further than talent."

Heart. That kid has heart.

Jack arrived early to every practice and every game. Just as he had in previous years, he spent most of the time on the bench. But this time his coach showed him how to play the game. He taught him strategy. He made him run drills. He instilled values in him, about sportsman-ship, and courage, and determination. Unlike some of Jack's previous coaches, Coach Tyler never yelled at the kids. He gave them firm, but gentle, direction. At games, he sat calmly in one of the chairs against the wall. When his team would start to lose ground, he didn't pace and freak out on them. He would stand up and put his hands in his pockets. That's how you knew he was nervous.

That season, Jack didn't only pass the ball.

He missed the basket more times than he made it, but when Coach Tyler said, "Shoot!" he listened.

He tried harder.

He kept at it.

He took more chances.

Then, about a month into the season, Coach Tyler told him, "I'm moving you up to the gold team."

The gold team had A-players, and the team won every game that season. They also won the county championship. Jack only played for two minutes in that game, but he was part of it. He was part of it because he has heart. And sometimes, heart is more important than talent.

Heart plus coaching? That will make any willing player better. Heart plus coaching plus practice? Well, that's an unstoppable force.

After that winning season, Jack decided to be great at basketball.

I don't know when it happened, but at some point, he made a plan. He didn't tell us about it. He just started practicing. After school in the gym. At the court in the playground. In our driveway. He watched videos about how to run drills to get a better vertical. To get stronger. To get faster. He studied legends. He learned about optimal performance. He spent all summer playing basketball. Every single day.

When eighth grade started, he got up before school to go to the local gym to work out. He asked for compression garments to wear outside in winter months. Before he went to bed at night, he shot two hundred baskets. In the cold. In the rain. In the snow.

When it came time for new season, my wife, Polly, took him to his first practice.

Later that night, she said, "Um . . . something happened."

Oh god.

"Did he get cut?" I asked.

"No. Jack is . . . really good at basketball."

Wait, what?

"Like, he's a beast on the court," she added.

I wasn't sure what to make of what she said, and since taking him to practice didn't fit my work schedule that month, I had to wait until the first game of the season to find out for myself.

That day, I took a seat on one of the folding chairs along the side-lines, just as I always did. I glanced around the gym and then settled on the players' chairs lined up along the opposite wall. Lawrence. Tyrell. Andre. Conner. Huh. No Jack.

Polly sat down next to me and handed me her coffee to hold while she took off her jacket.

"I don't see him," I said. "Is he in the bathroom?"

She smiled and pointed at the court. "Look."

Oh! He's playing.

Wait. He's starting.

Wait. Wait. Wait. He's playing center.

"What's going on?" I loud-whispered to her.

She beamed. "I told you. He's really good."

That game, I clapped so loudly I hurt my hands. My wife was right: Jack was a beast. With fixed determination, he ran up and down that court, blocked shots, got rebound after rebound, and scored.

Okay. He's not messing around.

Jack had transformed himself from a nervous player, into a medi-ocre player, into a good player. And now, could he be a great player?

That season, Jack's team fought hard. They had a mixed group of different abilities and heights, so they won a few games and lost more than a few games. When it came time for the playoffs, I hoped they'd at least win a couple.

Maybe they'll come in fourth. That would be good.

The important thing was, he'd shown up for the season how he wanted to play—for himself. He'd played well in in every game.

They won the first game of the playoffs. *Awesome. At least they advanced one time.*

They won the second game. *Look at that! A good way to finish the season.*

And the third. *Huh.*

They'll lose the fourth game for sure. The players on that team are too good. That's okay. Totally acceptable. They had a heck of a season.

Except.

Except Jack was determined.

He was on a mission.

For that fourth game, Jack built up each member of the team with encouragement. He compelled them to try harder, move faster, push, push, push.

And they won.

Against a better team that had had a better season, they *won*.

When we showed up for the championship game, I still couldn't believe they'd done it. Now it was down to two teams, and one of those teams hadn't lost a game all season: Coach Tyler's team. Yes, Jack had to play against his former teammates and his former coach.

Electric energy filled the school gym. Behind me in the sidelines, parents placed bets on Coach Tyler's team to win. They were probably right. Who could beat them? From watching every one of Jack's previous season games, I knew Coach Tyler's strategy involved going easy in the first half and then pulling out big energy in the final quarter. Our guys were exhausted from playing four games in the playoffs, which they didn't expect to win.

Well, no one but Jack.

At the first buzzer, I gripped my coffee cup so hard the top popped off.

Jack faced off against Carlos, the star player from the other team.

Until the half, the teams were neck and neck.

Six–ten.

Fourteen–twelve.

Eighteen–sixteen.

In the third quarter, just as I expected, Coach Tyler's team kicked into overdrive. They started to pick up points.

Eighteen–twenty-two.

Eighteen–twenty-eight.

Eighteen–thirty.

With less than four minutes left in the game, Jack's team was now twelve points behind. The kids were tired. They were losing ground.

Then the beast awakened.

"Let's go! Let's do this!" Jack shouted to his teammates.

He got the rebound and raced down the court. Swish. Two points.

The other team missed.

Rebound. Go!

Swish. Two points.

Rebound.

Again.

Again.

Jack scored another six points in under a minute.

Twenty-six–thirty.

His teammates picked up four more.

Coach Tyler stood up and put his hands in his pockets.

In the final minute, the game was tied up, thirty–thirty.

We were on our feet, our shouts drowned out by deafening cheers.

Then Coach Tyler's team scored a three-pointer.

Damn.

Damn.

That's it, then.

Except.

Except this kid was a beast.

He played every game with heart, even when he didn't have the skills.

He transformed himself from a bench-warmer to a player in a matter of months.

Drills. Morning workouts. Practice. And two hundred shots in the driveway.

He was on a mission.

Jack's teammate ran it down. Three points!

Thirty-three–thirty-three.

My wife paced. She couldn't look.

And then, two feet off the ground, Jack blocked a shot.

He ran it down court.

Swish.

They won.

They won!

Stunned, we congratulated Jack after the game and hugged him way too long.

That day, Jack didn't want to stand longer for pictures, so I took a few snaps and then, as usual, went to wait for him in the car.

Walking out of the gym, I was in lockstep with Coach Tyler.

"Good game," I said. "I want to thank you, so much, for helping Jack learn how to be a better player. For seeing that he had heart."

Coach Tyler smiled and, without missing a step, said, "I hate that kid."

You don't need talent.

It's okay if you weren't the best writer in class.

It's a craft. You can get better at it.

You don't need talent. You need *heart*.

Heart and *practice*.

Dribble. Pass. Shoot. Rebound. Defense.

Reader First. Core Message. A Promise you can deliver.

Sprint. Sprint again. Again. And again.

Two hundred shots in the driveway. Two hundred words before dawn.

Try again. Make it better. Simplify.

Refocus. Back to basics.

Core Message.

Promise.

Reader First.

Show up. Sprint. Show up. Sprint.

Sprint again.

Edit. Make it better.

Make it better again.

Don't give up.

Awaken the beast.

Write. Write. Write.

That season will be burned in my memory forever. To see my son work so hard for something and make it happen, to play for the love of the game, for the joy of it, was remarkable. I have the same feeling when I see my authors finish their books—their *damn good* books. And when they publish those damn good books, well—that's next-level joy. Know why? Because I'm not just happy and excited for them; I'm happy and excited for their readers. My authors rock worlds. They light the way forward on dark and precarious paths. They walk people into bright and beautiful futures. They really do change lives.

That's you, too, now.

Throughout this book, you've heard me refer to "my authors" dozens of times. Now you're one of them. Because you did the work. Because you put your reader first. Because you showed up for them, and for you.

You're not just "writing a book." You're an author.

You understand your reader. You know how to craft a compelling Core Message and a Promise you can deliver. You know how to filter your content and create an outline that respects the Reader Journey. You know how to do practical stuff, like plan how long it will take you to write your first draft. And you know how to do messy stuff, like surrender to the creative process and actually write the thing. You're an editing warrior with a proven system that will take your manuscript to new levels of awesome. You're a better storyteller. And you're a better advocate for your reader and for yourself.

You did the hard work, and then you did it again.

Screw talent. *You know how to write a must-read book.*

And that means you can do it—not only once, but again and again, if you wish. So that brings me to my big question: What will you write next? Now that you're an author, how will you serve the world with your body of work?

Onward!

I'll see you on the shelves.

Acknowledgments

I HAVE A PET PEEVE about acceptance speeches at award shows. It's not that most of them are boring and the winners ramble on. It's that almost everyone thanks their spouse or partner last—often while the orchestra is playing their "get the hell off the stage, this show is already an hour over" music.

If you're lucky enough to have someone who supports you through the creation of something from nothing—a movie, a TV show, a book— you better damn well thank them *first*. Having a person who believes in you gives you a huge advantage, and let's face it, that's why you won. Hell, that's probably how you found the courage to start your project in the first place, let alone finish it, submit it, and send it out into the world.

My wife, Polly, gets top billing in these here acknowledgments. Without her, this book quite literally would not exist. Writers can be infuriatingly singular-focused and insecure. Projects always take longer than predicted. We need a ridiculous amount of alone time and an endless supply of reassurance. By some miracle, I married a person who decided I was worth all that. Thank you, my love, for all the things.

We have a family motto: Show up for the people you love. The people *I love* have shown up for me in big ways. I dedicated this book to my son, Jack, because he inspires me to go after what I want, no matter how the odds are stacked against me. His father, Patrick, has that same spirit and has believed in me since we were kids sitting on my father's dock, making wishes on stars. I'm blessed with parents who valued blazing a trail over following a well-trodden path. Nicki and Jerry never asked me to dim my light or water down my dreams, and I'm so grateful.

I'm also lucky to have a wonderful chosen family of friends who never suggested I shelve an idea or choose a practical vocation. The idea for this book came to me while on vacation on Madeline Island, so thank you to my "island family." A special thanks to my lifelong pal, the brilliant poet and editor Zoë Bird, who helped me edit this book.

At the center of my work family is Mike Michalowicz. To me, he is more than my writing partner—he's my brother. If Mike hadn't called BS on me all those years ago, I wouldn't have bothered to break down my process and teach it to others. Many people know his business acumen, his goofy ways, and his hustle, yet it's Mike's kind, loyal, and generous heart that means the most to me. Mike, I'm so proud of the work we have done together, and I can't wait for the next ten (or is it more?) books.

We all have a short list of people we'd say "yes" to without question, and Amber Vilhauer is at the top of mine. We came up in this business together and I couldn't be more grateful for her friendship and collaboration over the years. She is the genius behind the launch of this book and so many others you know and love. Amber, thank you so much for your hard work on this project.

Ten thousand thanks to a member of my work family, my "ride or die" right hand, Laura Stone. She kept the embers burning for this book even when I was sure I'd never finish it. She "mom'd" this book into existence. Laura, thank you for your integrity, your loyalty, and for all your hard work helping me get this book into the hands of as many authors as possible.

I am fortunate to have a community of work colleagues who have become dear friends. Thank you to everyone who encouraged me to teach and to write this book, especially my think-outside-the-box business coach, Andrea Lee; self-employment visionary, Jeffrey

Shaw; life reinvention expert, Kristina Paider; and brilliant storyteller, Julian Winters.

Thank you to my publisher, Page Two. The entire team at has been lovely and ever so patient with me, despite my many delays. I think they thought they were getting a pro who wouldn't cause them grief or frustration. (Psych!) This pro had a heck of a time finishing this book, and I appreciate your unwavering support and positivity. Thank you to my editor, Amanda Lewis; my project coordinator, Adrineh Der-Boghossian; Meghan O'Neill in marketing; my designer, Peter Cocking; and my ever-patient copy editor, Tilman Lewis. A special note of gratitude to Trena White, who has been so gracious to me and to the Top Three author family.

Deep thanks to Michael and Amy Port of Heroic Public Speaking who helped me find the courage to step out from behind the curtain and share my own voice. Maybe that was their plan all along. I'll never know, because they're classy like that. Michael and Amy, your confidence in me helped make this book possible. I am honored to be part of *your* work family.

Thank you to my advance readers for taking the time to read an early vision of this book and share your honest feedback with me.

Last, but certainly not least, thank you to my Top Three Book Workshop authors. You care so much about your readers, and it shows. You stand for excellence and meet every challenge head on. And you support each other in meaningful ways. I'm endlessly proud of you and I'm honored to know you.

Index

advance on royalties, 220, 226, 227
agents, 225–26
Anderson, Julie, 125
The Artist's Way (Cameron), 108, 135
authors, fiction, 7–8

Baker, Dr. Bob, 108–9
Barber, Sue, 158, 159, 160
Bird by Bird (Lamott), 115
Book Yourself Solid (Port), 4
books: abandoned, 1–2, 183; authors,
    success of, 3; beating the odds, 161–62;
    "better business card," 1, 2, 3, 5, 6, 171;
    Content Filter, 75–92; Core Message,
    45–61; editing, Must-Read Method,
    149–63; first draft, 115–30; friction
    edit, 183–94; front-load the message,
    99; Ideal Reader, 25–44; inner critic,
    45, 73–74, 105, 121, 131–46; introduc-
    tion vs. Chapter 1, 95–97; promise and
    deliver, 63–74; publishing, 215–32;
    reader as protagonist, 94–95; reader
    connection edit, 175–82; reader
    engagement edit, 195–202; reader
    feedback, 203–14; Reader First, 9–22;
    the Reader Journey, 16, 95, 102–3,
166–68, 169, 172, 177; reader trans-
    formation edit, 165–74; the Reader's
    Epiphany, 103–6; Table of Contents,
    109; trade review, 159–60; transfor-
    mational outlines, 93–112. *See also*
    Harper, Anjanette (AJ)
Briggs, John, 51–52

Cameron, Julia, 108, 135
Campbell, Joseph, 10, 102
Casablanca, 28
The Chicago Manual of Style, 189, 209
Ciavolino, Mike, 59–60
Clockwork (Michalowicz), 4, 208
Compton, Kasey, 176–77
Content Filter: connect with reader, 81;
    creating structure, 77; deliver the
    Promise, 82–83; interviews, 85–
    88; manage information overload,
    75–77; narrative composition (stories,
    anecdotes, case studies), 78–81;
    protecting content, 89–90; support
    core message, 82; teaching points,
    77–78, 92, 172; working content,
    90–92; workshop, build content
    inventory, 83–85

For information on writing
and editing workshops, go to
ajharper.com

For free tools and
milestone rewards, go to
writeamustread.com

About the Author

AJ HARPER is an editor and publishing strategist who helps authors write transformational books that enable them to build readership, grow their brand, and make a significant impact on the world. As ghostwriter and as developmental editor, AJ has worked with newbies to *New York Times*–bestselling authors with millions of books sold. Through her fourteen-week live course, Top Three Book Workshop, AJ helps authors write, edit, and publish game-changing books.

In addition to her work in nonfiction, AJ has edited more than ninety novels. On a mission to change the landscape for LGBTQ+ stories, she co-founded a traditional publishing house, Interlude Press/ Duet Books, which went on to win numerous awards and critical acclaim, and launched the careers of several prominent Young Adult authors. Chicago Review Press acquired Interlude in 2022.

AJ helped design the speech development program for Heroic Public Speaking. For TEDxCambridge, she has coached renowned economic research scientists from Harvard, Yale, MIT, and the World Economic Forum.

AJ is writing partner to business author Mike Michalowicz. Together they've written nine books, including *The Pumpkin Plan, Profit First, Clockwork, Fix This Next,* and *Get Different.*

A born-and-raised Minnesota "lake" girl, AJ lives in New York with her wife and son. Connect with her at ajharper.com.